SELF LOVE

A Silent Revolution

Thank you for supporting my healing journey with love

[signature]

QUANIECE RAQUELLE

2020 by Quaniece Jones

...niece Jones in Partnership with The
...iterary Revolutionary
...v.theliteraryrevolutionary.com

Editing By: Anjé McLish
...ver Design By: Opeyemi Ikuborije
...ior Formatting By: Opeyemi Ikuborije

Publisher's Note:

Manufactured in the United States of America

ISBN #: 978-1-950279-23-4

Follow Quaniece!
Social Media Outlets:
@withlovequaniece_

CONTENTS

Dedication

Acknowledgments

Preface

Hate it or Love it 1

The Value of Eve 9

The Mother is our First Home 11

Mercy 19

Childhood Trauma 23

I Am Woman 31

Black Girl Goals 35

Nothing Real Can Be Threatened 39

Faith Over Fear 45

Daddy Issues 49

You Can't Pour From an Empty Vessel 59

We are all connected 63

Therapy for a Black Girl... 69

Talk to Me Nice.. 75

God's Plan 79

Luv Drought 87

Never Let Me Drown... 97

New Balance 103

Speak 111

Only The Guilty Get Offended............................... 123

Favor Ain't Fair.. 125

Dedication

I dedicate this book to my beautiful mahogany Queen, "my mother." The woman who no matter what always put her family first. I thank God for blessing me with a mother like you every day and for knowing that in your care, I would grow into everything that he planned for my life. I am strong because of you. I am resilient because of you. I am an amazing mother because of you. Because you did, I can.

Acknowledgments

First and foremost I would like to thank God. Without you I am nothing.

To Ashanti, my love, my best friend, my balance, the yin to my yang, thank you for your endless support of my journey, growth, and healing. You see me, and I love you for that.

To Chance, Mommy loves you so much. I spent many nights writing with your head on my chest. I want you to know that you have the power to do and be anything you want in life. Mommy will always have your back.

To my Nana, you have always instilled in me the importance of helping others. You travel all across this country sharing your testimony, I love that and I love you.

To Nayda Lemay, my therapist, there are no words to be able to thank you for how you have contributed to my healing. You have encouraged me and supported me as if I was your own daughter. I thank God for you being in my life. I have the best mentor in the world.

To my writing professors at Central Connecticut State University, Kathryn Zurlo, thank you for your endless words of encouragement and tips to make me a better writer. Dr. Catherine Baratta, I can hear your comments in my ear everytime I start a paper. This book was produced because you pushed me, without even knowing. Thank you. Dr. Yvonne Patterson, I fell in love with trauma because of your class. As a woman of color who beat the odds, you inspire me in so many ways, thank you.

Rickey "RJ" Flagg Jr., my best friend, thank you for always supporting me and loving me. You question everything but when it comes to me you show up no questions asked and I love you deeply for that.

To the gang Tiff and Forty, I LOVE Y'ALL. Miami Squad Forever. Highland Gang Forever.

To Rich, I will never forget all those conversations we had about our childhood and wanting to be better for our children. You opened my eyes and heart to the pain of the black man and I will forever be grateful.

To Nia and the entire team at The Literary Revolutionary & Co, I prayed for each and every one of you. I am honored to be a part of this movement.

Preface

They say women don't know the power and value they hold. I say, how could you know something that you were never taught? I don't think I had ever heard the term "self-love" until I was about twenty-one years old. I heard it after experiencing a major heartbreak that I couldn't seem to bounce back from. In the midst of my pain, I stumbled across my first self-help book, *Eat Pray Love* by Elizabeth Gilbert. After reading this book and hearing about this self-love phenomenon, I was hooked. I wanted to know more, I needed to know more. I thought I had finally found what was wrong with me and how I could fix it. In a way, I did—I just didn't know what all "fixing" entailed.

Reading has always been my favorite pastime, but I never read with purpose, or with intention. Which is probably why whenever I'd go searching for a good book, I'd walk right by the self-help section. By the time I discovered the genre of self-help, I had already made a ton of mistakes and experienced a series of pain. By the age of 21, I was tired. Tired of giving and never receiving. I was tired of leaving relationships with damn near nothing because I had given everything that I had to them. I was tired of this void that I felt. At this moment I made a decision, a decision that would change things forever. I decided to stop sitting back and wishing for a better life, but to activate the power within me and start doing something about it.

So, what does self-love mean? I am now twenty-eight years old, and I finally feel like I know what it means to love myself. Over the years, I have died and rebuilt myself so many times. It took many years of unlearning all that I was not before finally uncovering who I really am and then taking the time to learn and get to know and love this woman.

Not only did I have to learn how to love myself—I also had to forgive myself. I had to let go of the guilt for the things I didn't know. This had to be done before I could fully embrace my self-love. At this point, I am not only aware of what self-love means, but I am implementing self-love into all aspects of my life.

Growing up as a young black woman, love and healthy relationships are two things I rarely talked about with my loved ones. Over the years, through interactions with my peers, I've learned in many of our household's discussions that this wasn't something often discussed. We knew our parents loved us because they provided for us, but positive images of a healthy loving relationship, let alone self-love, wasn't something that I was familiar with.

I always knew I was very intelligent. When I was in school, learning new things always came easy for me. But love? I was pretty screwed in that department and I was on a road going nowhere fast. Because of this, I began to study myself. My needs, patterns, my habits, my triggers, my own dysfunction. Year by year, I strived to be the best person I could be with or without a counterpart. This process was very painful, and I often felt as if I was at war with myself.

Love and I had a very up and down relationship, so to say. Even when I told myself I didn't want love, deep down I really did. I'd convinced myself to give love a try, but each time I kept getting hurt and I just couldn't understand why. I blamed love for my heartache and pain. I convinced myself that love did nothing but cause hurt, pain, and trouble. I was so desperate, when a person showed me they "loved" me, I did any and everything to keep that love. Sometimes that meant hurting others in the process, but the majority of the time it meant ruining myself. My idea of love became so obscured that it was no longer a requirement for those around me to love me back. I was okay with giving, never believing that I deserved the same love I would selflessly give.

My journey to self-love turned into me trying to prove to others that I was worthy of love. In the past, I never received love without someone wanting something from me in return. I began to be an excessive giver. I believed if I gave and gave, then one day I would eventually find someone who loved me and would give back to me. When I was rejected, instead of letting go, I wanted to change their mind. I needed to prove to myself that after so many times of being hurt that I was still lovable. Not even knowing that the person that needed that love the most was me.

Hate it or Love it

It's hard to love yourself properly when you don't know who you are or who God is in your life—when you don't recognize him as your creator. When you know God and you know how much he loves you and how important you are, the way you feel about yourself will transform. After learning and affirming who God said I was, my self-love and confidence began to increase little by little, day by day. It took years to get to that point, and even longer before I actually believed in my testimony and that it was valuable enough to help someone. I didn't write this book to be cute. I wrote it with the intention of saving lives, to free young girls like me from years of suffering and living a life filled with bondage, presently and in the future.

I grew up seeing the women around me putting their needs and wants behind those of the people they chose to love. These women sacrificed their values and morals in exchange for having someone around to say they loved them. So, I guess you can say I subconsciously inherited that trait no matter how bad I didn't want it. When I began to develop relationships, I created a pattern of placing other's needs and feelings before my own, and in the process neglecting myself.

Over the years, I've heard several people say that if you loved yourself you wouldn't have allowed someone to hurt you, or treat you poorly. That statement made me feel even worse because I do love myself. In fact, I love myself more than anything in this world. However, my lack of boundaries paired with a lot of unresolved trauma kept me in a loop of toxic cycles and habits that unknowingly ran my life.

Having boundaries is necessary. Not having boundaries can be detrimental, not only to you, but also to everything that you are attached to or have worked hard to obtain. Lack of boundaries can affect you in the workplace. It can affect the way you parent your children. The way you interact and deal with your family relationships. Not having boundaries invites all kinds of turmoil in your life. Have you ever heard the saying, *if you let stuff slide people will ice skate all over your entire life?* It's pretty self-explanatory, and it had become my entire life. I attended the school of no boundaries and graduated with a Doctorate degree. When you have no boundaries, you allow people to slowly steal you. Bit by bit and piece by piece, you will begin to lose more of yourself. One day, you'll look at yourself in the mirror and realize you have no idea who you are or how you got there. That was me, and that was one of the worst feelings I have ever felt in my life. I vowed that I would never feel that way again.

My story isn't a fairytale. There is no prince charming riding in on a white horse to save me or free me from my troubles or bad decisions. No one to sweep me off my feet and make me forget all the troubles I ever had to endure. The only man that has ever come to save me was Jesus Christ. This is my truth. This is my life. The things I am sharing with you are my real life experiences that I lived through and survived. These are some of my most vulnerable and painful truths. Real pain that I had to fight through in order to get to the other side of healing. What you're about to read is years and years of self-work, healing, prayer, and deliverance from God.

I am not some bitter woman who has given up on love and decided to be on my own forever so I will never have to experience pain again. This is about a woman who was so tired of being hurt and stepped over who finally took her power back. I absolutely still believe in love. I believe that there is a man on this earth who God created just for me. Who's going to love me exactly how I always wanted to be loved—with commitment, love, understanding, and respect. He will value me. He will walk to the edge with me. I will feel safe and secure.

I will be able to show up as my most authentic self. This love will liberate me, and motivate me to be the best person I can be. I want that kind of love that makes the world jealous. A love that will glorify God and people will look and say, that has to be God's blessing. I know in every relationship there will be hardships, but cheating, devaluing my feelings, and disrespecting me are not things that I believe are hardships. *Those are choices.* People either choose to treat you with love and respect or not.

One of my favorite quotes by the famous James Baldwin states, "Our crown has already been bought and paid for. All we have to do is wear it." Can you imagine that? It took so long for that to really settle in and make sense to me. As a perfectionist and over achiever, to know that there was nothing else more that I had to do to be deserving of God's love and grace was such a relief. To know that God loves me unconditionally. To know that there is nothing that I can do that will separate me from the love of God. Nothing. Only through God's forgiving love and grace was I able to survive.

For me to fully love myself, the way God loves each and every one of us, I had to make some major changes. I had to separate myself from some people I would have given my last in the name of love. On this journey I have experienced pain, doubt, shame, betrayal, and deceit. I have caused others pain. I can admit that at a point in my life I was very toxic. I'm not perfect, nor will I portray myself as a victim. I am a survivor. Have I done some horrible things in life? Yes. Have I allowed others to do some horrible things to me? Absolutely. When you are a hurt person, you hurt others. When you are lacking love internally, you will take a little piece of what anyone gives you. I'm a delivered people-pleaser, and I've spent *a lot* of time making others happy before myself. I've made a lot of decisions in life mostly with good intentions, but somehow still costing me my worth. I remember times feeling like I would be stuck forever, that I would never amount to anything or be worthy because of the things that I have allowed to happen. But I'm here as living proof to tell you that none of what you have been through is who you are. The past is just that—the past. Every day you get a choice—to change your mind, to change your situation, to change your life. You get a choice to forgive yourself, the same way God extends his grace and forgiveness. You get a choice to take all of that pain you had to endure and you use it as fuel—fuel to be a better you, fuel to find your purpose in life and allow yourself to experience joy. Don't ever think your negative experiences should count you out. In fact, you deserve it more. Why? Because you survived, and God never forgot or left you. That thing that you thought would kill you could be the very same thing that leads you to your purpose in life and closer to God, if you choose to keep moving forward.

Without God, I am nothing. I know that even when I feel alone, I'm not alone. I know that even though my past is flawed, God still loves me, and that he still walks with me daily. Even when I have put him on the back burner and got in my own way, I know that no matter what, he will never leave me nor forsake me. God's grace has saved my life. God saved me from myself. Through God's love, I learned what my worth was and the value that I hold. I learned that I am the head and not the tail. I have accepted that I am not for everyone, and I'm finally okay with that. The only person I now strive to please is God. I no longer care about being liked or having my feelings validated, especially by a bunch of people who don't even like themselves. My testimony will reach the people that God intended to receive this message. When I am dead and gone, I will leave behind my words, my experiences, and most importantly my desire to serve and a heart that always wanted to help. No matter how many beatings it took, my pain is a gift, my testimony is a gift to you all. To learn from my mistakes. God has a way of making sure you receive what you are supposed to receive when you are supposed to receive it. I'm a strong beautiful young black woman who has God by her side, for that reason alone I *cannot* be stopped. For a long time, I denied myself of God's love. I believed that due to the things that happened, I was unworthy and there was no way God would even want to hear from me. I know that even today I'm still not perfect and I never will be. I am flawed, yet I am still perfect in his eyes. I know that I still fail him daily, but I refuse to allow that fear to keep me away from him. The devil is a liar, and God still loves me in spite of ALL that. He loves each and every one of you all with the same unconditional love. God's love is only *for* you, never against you. His love is limitless. Only you can deny yourself of that. I am honored and blessed to be sharing my story and lessons with you all. Use my trials and tribulations as a guide to navigate your own. I hope this story touches someone's life. Thank you.

The Value of Eve

"This is now bone of my bones and flesh of my flesh; she shall be called 'woman', for she was taken out of man." -
Genesis 2:23

How is it that even in one of today's oldest sources of information—the Bible, which clearly states woman was taken and created from man—women including myself have taken this and done the complete opposite? Even minimizing the value we have within ourselves and somehow behaving the complete opposite to what God has purposed for our existence?

One day, I stumbled across a radio interview by Devon Franklin. He was on tour promoting the release of a new book and he started an interesting conversation about the significance of Eve being created from Adam. In this text it states Adam felt alone. He felt incomplete. He felt as if something was missing from him. Nowhere in this text did God say Eve felt incomplete without Adam, nor was she even looking for him. When Adam saw Eve, he knew that she was a good thing, that she was a part of him, and what he had been missing. She had value and was more precious than rubies. I started thinking, where along the lines did that get misconstrued?

In my own experience, I have loved hard—so hard, I even compromised my self-worth and value to come down to where a man was versus requiring him to come up to reach my level. I am already who God created me to be. He gave me the values and assets needed to have a successful, loving healthy relationship if I choose. But instead, we live in a culture that focuses on women and what we should and shouldn't be to keep and maintain a man. This leaves us feeling worthless, objectified and devalued. As women, it feels wrong when we go against our intuition or stay in situations that are not aligned with who we are. Like when we tolerate less than what we deserve in the name of love. This narrative gives love such a bad reputation. When it is not love that it is the issue. It is the lack of love within ourselves, that manifests to a man fulfilling what we lack internally. We sit and wait forever to be full. I don't know about you but for me it never came. No matter how well I was loved or treated, none of it mattered because the void I was looking to fill could only be filled by God. Love heals. It liberates. It unites where there is division. It brings understanding when there is chaos. Love is the most powerful source. For *God* is love.

The Mother is our First Home

"But behind all your stories is always your mother's story, because hers is where yours begins." –Mitch Albom

The foundation you grow up on is so crucial to how you will function and interact in your adult life. The things you see, the relationships around you, the habits you formed— all contribute to your development as a person, and which values and beliefs you learn, intentionally and unintentionally. Your environment and upbringing has a direct effect on the way you will one day function in society. I'm sure we have all heard the term being a "product" of our environment. From experience I've learned that even when growing up in the most ideal environment, everyone faces their own trials and tribulations. We are on this earth to learn and evolve and to experience. God uses each of us for a very specific reason. You can lean in and hear the voice, or choose to ignore it. Either way, life will continue to happen. As you begin to open up your eyes and observe what is going on around you, you will see that nothing is by accident. Nothing.

I grew up in a small town called Windsor, Connecticut. My mother is a registered nurse. My father is an ex-convicted felon who served over ten years in a federal prison from my teenage years to early adulthood. He was in and out of jail most of my life, so our relationship was pretty much nonexistent from the start. My mother left my father when I was two years old. I have no recollection of them ever being together. I think I remember seeing one picture of them together as a couple. My mother gave birth to me at the age of 17 years old, and she raised me without my father's help, and she never complained about it or badmouthed him.

As far back as I can remember, it was always me and my mom. We always had a close relationship. We always did everything together. We basically grew up together. Life has a way of showing you how your relationships with the people closest to you are often tested during your trials and tribulations—and theirs as well.

Growing up, my mother was hardworking and ambitious. My childhood was filled with my mother working and going to school to be able to provide a better life for me . I never went without. As I think back on my childhood, I often asked myself what more could I have wanted? My mother provided for me and gave me everything that I ever thought I needed. It took me many many years to realize that some of the things I needed couldn't be bought. I desired affection. I desired love. I desired words of encouragement and praise. But my mother, like myself, had no idea what that entailed. Seeing as she was also a product of her environment, she never received it. Before I pieced that together, I harbored anger inside of me for a very long time. I was angry with my mom, but a part of me knew it was something that she never intended to do. After much therapy and processing what I felt, I was able to release that anger. I know now that she only did what she thought was right with the knowledge and resources she had. My mother did the best that she could with what she had. I will forever be grateful for the mother that God chose to guide me in this life.

My mother is a powerhouse—a force to be reckoned with. She does not play at all. She is the epitome of strength. What she lacked in nurturing, she made up with drive and ambition. I watched my mother bust her behind and build a stable life from the bottom up. My mother is the reason I am resilient, why I am strong and ambitious. Anything that I put my mind to, I execute, and I learned that from my mom. My mother wasn't supposed to make it. My mother grew up during the crack epidemic, a time that many African Americans didn't make it out. Black families have never been the same. My mother had me at 17 years old by a drug dealer and became addicted to drugs after my father was sent off to prison. Even though she saw and experienced horrible things while I was a baby, my mother knew that she still wanted more. She didn't let her circumstances stop her. She had a desire to be better than what she was. My mother did any and everything she could to make sure that happened.

By the grace of God, my mother has been clean for over 25 years. Through Narcotics Anonymous, my mother was delivered from her addiction and her faith in God allowed her to stay clean. The strength she developed through this program is remarkable. The twelve steps are all built and founded on a relationship with higher power. Not only did my mother set an example for me, but for her own mother. Her journey inspired my grandmother to get clean as well. I come from a long line of addicts. Addiction is one of the generational curses that affected my family's ability to move forward. My grandfather, my mother's father, was also an addict. He died from HIV when I was four months old. He died in 1991, when people didn't have much information on the virus, just that it guaranteed death. My father's mother was also an addict, but didn't die of drugs; she died of breast cancer when I was five years old. Of course, I had my own struggles with addiction. Weed was my choice of drug. As hard as this is for me to write, I still struggle with this, especially during periods of high stress. I used weed as a way to cope with my anxiety and unresolved trauma for many years. This isn't much different from the millions of Americans struggling and suffering from anxiety, depression, and post-traumatic stress disorder using antipsychotics and antidepressants. We are in pain. Many of us are suffering from unresolved trauma manifesting in many other areas. With the Opioid Epidemic at an all-time high, it is no coincidence that more and more people have become dependent on medications just to function in everyday life.

I'll never forget the last time I saw my paternal grandmother before she passed away. Seeing my grandmother before she died is the last memory I have of her. My Nana, my mother's mom, drove me down to Savannah, Georgia to see my grandma. My father's family had called my mom and told her that my grandmother was dying of breast cancer, and she wasn't going to make it much longer. My Nana, also being from the south, didn't mind bringing me to see my grandmother. I remember walking the long halls in a hospital-style building and walking into the room to see my grandmother lying in bed. I was afraid. I was five years old and I had never seen someone dying before. She looked so weak, she could barely speak. I remember my aunts giving her sips of water and ice chips as the head of the bed was raised. Although my grandmother's physical condition was deteriorating by the minute, I just remember her eyes and the way she looked at me. Her eyes were so bright when she saw me. I don't remember much about my grandmother before that, but from what my mom always told me she was crazy about me, her grand-baby. I knew in that moment looking into her eyes, she loved me. I felt it. I knew that me being there made her happy, and although she couldn't verbalize it, I felt her love, and I will never forget it. I know in my heart that my grandmother is watching over me, guiding me, and protecting me. My angel.

After driving back home with my Nana and arriving at my house, my mother had called my aunts down south to let them know that we had gotten back home safely. It was then that we received the news that my grandmother had passed away the night I saw her last. A part of me always felt that she was waiting for me to leave because she didn't want me to see her die. I felt like before I got there, she was holding on because she wanted to see me one last time. I gave her that peace she needed to leave this earth. I will forever be grateful.

Mercy

*"[Mercy] is the concern for the physical as well as spiritual
need of those who are hurting. Those with this gift have
great empathy for others in their trials and sufferings. They
are able to come alongside people over extended periods of
time and see them through their healing process." -
Natasha Heath*

Narcotics Anonymous (NA) is an international community based organization for individuals who are recovering addicts. Members of this group learn from one another on how to live drug free and recover from the effects of addiction. As a kid, I went to several NA meetings with my mom and Nana. When my Nana got clean, my family always made me go with her when she went out so she could stay clean. They knew that if I was there she would be less likely to get in trouble if she had someone there holding her accountable. I look back on that now and think about how at such a young age, I had such a great responsibility to take care of the people around me. I actually should have just been somewhere being a child. I believe that growing up in this environment cultivated my passion for helping others, healing, and therapy. I am currently a full time student obtaining my undergraduate degree in Social Work. Or maybe this passion was always there. Maybe God put me in this specific family to develop the gifts he placed inside of me before I was in my mother's womb. I need you to know that nothing is by accident. God has a plan for your life in good times and in bad; trust in him.

At these meetings, I would listen to horrible things people have done at the expense of being on drugs. I grew up listening to their stories, too young to comprehend the impact that drugs had on so many people's lives. You never know what people are going through or what they have been through. You can never judge a person by how they look on the outside. For some reason, these stories that I listened to resonated with me. I was curious about this God person I kept hearing about. Hearing people talk about God and how he helped them get over something that was created to physically take over your entire body is still a miracle to me. I know now that this environment was connected to the purpose that God placed on my life. Have mercy. God blessed me with the gift of mercy. He's blessed you with gifts too. My upbringing formed my perception of how I viewed the world and people—with love and care. I knew from an early age that people were hurting and struggling in this world. For as long as I can remember, I have been the friend that people go to and tell their most shameful truths and secrets. I have the ability to make people feel seen and heard and loved—no matter how bad the choices they made—because no matter how bad it may sound, I still look at them with love. Deep down inside, I have always believed that there is a way out of any situation. I know now that with God, all things are possible—even the most impossible situation is for God to show you his power. God does this for all of us. He doesn't care about what we did or where we came from. God sent his only son Jesus Christ to Earth to die so each and every one of us could live. Jesus was the ultimate sacrifice. Because Jesus died for us, there is nothing that can separate us from God's love. So for those of you who are reading this book and don't know how significant Jesus is dying and rising up three days later, let me break it down for you.

God created laws, but God also knew we would fail over and over again. But because he loved us so much, he sent the only son he had to Earth. Jesus was perfect. *He* was created in the image of God. People still hated him. They still were cruel to him. They killed him and tortured him. He faced many trials and tribulations the same way we face them every day. He had opposition. Even after witnessing his power and what it could do, they still hated him. But because he knew who he was, who he belonged to, and what he had been called to earth to do, he let them do and say whatever they wanted. He loved his enemies. He prayed for them. He healed them. He blessed his enemies even when he knew that they would betray him. Talk about having *character*. God created each and every one of us in his image. Which means that in his eyes, we are perfect. We are fearfully and wonderfully made.

Childhood Trauma

When I was five years old, I was molested by my older cousin who was sixteen. It was a sunny summer afternoon. I was wearing a black and white checkered shirt with yellow sunflowers over black shorts. I remember going outside and playing in the sprinklers at the park across the street. I didn't know that by the end of the day, my life would never be the same again. I came inside the house from playing outside and I went to the bathroom. I remember him peeking in and looking at me. He told me to come into the room when I was done, so I did. No one was watching us, so for the brief period of us being unaccounted for, no one noticed. He locked the door behind him and showed me his penis. It was disgusting. I remember feeling grossed out. I remember him laying me on my back and pulling my underwear down, and then putting his mouth on my vagina. My cousin saw an opportunity to make himself feel powerful and he took it. One moment changed my entire life. One moment shaped the way I would view myself for the next twenty years. One moment robbed me of my innocence.

Even when I thought this didn't have an effect on me, it did.

As a child, I knew what he was doing to me was wrong. I am so proud of myself for being a five-year-old little girl with the courage to tell someone. I am also proud of the twenty-eight-year-old woman who found the courage to tell this story again, this time with the intention and hope sharing my story will give you the courage to share yours. Your story may not look like mine. It may seem small or big compared to mine. Regardless, it is still valid because it is yours and you have overcome it. That means that God still has his hand on you and there is still something that he needs to fulfill through you. Even though what you may have experienced was horrible and hurt so much, God has the power to turn the entire situation around—and he will. But you have to invite him in. Invite him into the painful, horrible experience. He wants you to call on him. He's waiting on *you*.

The relationship I had with my mother was very open. She talked about a lot of things with me and I knew that I could tell her anything. I told my mom one night when she was dropping me off at my aunt's house so she could go to work. I told her that I didn't ever want to go back to my grandmother's house because my cousin had touched me in a way that she told me was wrong. Telling my mother what had happened to me was very hard. I went back and forth inside of my head for days. I knew my mother was crazy and would do anything to protect me. I was scared for my cousin, but that feeling in my gut wouldn't go away. I know now that that was my intuition. At the age of 5, I just knew something was wrong, and I needed to tell someone that I could trust and she believed me. Fast forward to our present day, so many women are coming forward revealing rapes, sexual assaults, and harassment from years and years ago. To any person reading this book who has not told anyone of the violation you experienced: I don't care how long ago it was or who you feel that you have to protect—you did not deserve what happened to you. As I say this to you, I say this to my younger self. You did nothing wrong. You did not ask for it, and under no circumstances is the violation of one's body ever right. _None_. To the women and men who have sat and suffered in silence: you matter. Your life matters. Your well-being matters. Your existence matters. You are still worthy no matter what has happened to you. God still loves you and you are still qualified.

For so very long, I carried around the shame of my molestation, believing the lies the enemy told me daily—that what happened to me was my fault, that I deserved it. I asked for it. I was being grown. It was the way I was dressed. I shouldn't have been so silly and outgoing, then he would have never paid any attention to me to hurt me. I spent the rest of my youth trying to go unnoticed and unseen. Growing up, I never wanted to call any extra attention to myself because that attention usually came with pain. I was afraid of attracting the wrong people, so I hid. That shame followed me for many years. The shame that comes with being sexually violated is a fight I fought internally for a long time. Even when I thought it didn't affect me, it did. As a parent, it scares me every day when my child is out of my sight, because I know what I experienced. It was at the hands of family, who are the first people in your lives that are supposed to love you, take care of you, and protect you.

My mom reported the issue to the authorities. I'm not sure what exactly happened legally, but I remember my mom and I going to therapy. I remember during a session they told me that I was being recorded, and they gave me these little dolls. They told me to show them what had happened to me and I did. I remember the therapist asking me would I be able to go speak about it in a courtroom. By then, I was too afraid. It was one thing to tell my mother, but to go stand up in front of people that I didn't know? I couldn't do it. So I told my mom and the therapist that he didn't just do it to me.

He did it to my little cousin as well, which was true. I thought maybe she would be brave enough to be able to say it happened to her too, then I wouldn't have had to go through that alone. When her mother was told what had happened to me and that it had happened to her daughter as well, she asked her about it. She denied that anything had ever happened. The case got thrown out due to lack of evidence. Another predator was set free. And another little girl was left to pick up the pieces of what was left of her heart.

My molestation affected me in several different ways over the years. The physical harm from being sexually abused can never compare to the way the abuse affected me psychologically. Those times that I thought that I was healed when in reality the truth was I couldn't feel anything. I was numb. In response to the trauma that I experienced, I buried the anger I was carrying so deep on the inside of me. I buried that anger because I felt like I didn't have a right to be angry. Maybe I deserved what happened to me. For several years to come I endured so many painful situations, relationships, and friendships, without ever complaining because I felt like that's what I deserved. Who would ever want someone who was molested? I didn't even want myself. I can recall dating several guys in high school. Most of the time, it didn't go anywhere. Some I wanted to have sex with, some I didn't. I just knew that the male attention that I received, I liked. I wasn't getting the attention at home that I needed. My mom was busy trying to build a foundation, and my dad was hours away at a federal prison. When I gave my body away it made me feel powerful. Giving my body away gave me the power that I lacked in real life.

This desire for attention accompanied, with the inability to say no and a spirit of people-pleasing, was a formula for disaster. I often got into situations that most of the time I didn't know how to get out. Whether it was a guy forcing himself on me cause I decided to go chill with him alone, or having sex with someone that I never wanted to have sex with. I didn't feel like I had the right to say no. It was only after getting saved and dedicating my life to Christ that I find my identity. God's love showed me that what happened to me is not who I am— that I didn't have to carry the shame of what happened to me. He showed me that I was still worthy and his promises still applied to me.

After being molested, I counted myself out, but God still counted me in. I thought God left me, but he still had his hands on me. I thought that I was an embarrassment to God. When I looked into the mirror and hated what I saw, God still saw his beautiful creation and he still had a plan for my life. For every person I slept with, I never got a life threatening disease. My ability to have children still remained. I am beyond blessed, and even on my worst day, I have alway had what I needed and wanted. He never held one thing back from me with my ugly past.

The fact that I am writing this book to you is a test of my testimony. I had to push this book out of me. It didn't just come. I had to push past those feelings of fear, doubt and shame. Through spending quality time with God and developing an intimate relationship with him, I was able to believe that on the other side of fear is victory. This book is my victory. The enemy has done everything he could to stop me from getting this book out with every distraction, every obstacle he could throw my way. Even with the attacks on my mind, even those trying to attack me through my child and loved ones, I won't quit. The enemy is going so hard up against me so that I would give up and not birth what God has placed inside of me because this book is going to save many lives. I have faith that this book will reach so many women who are now or have been in the same place that I was—lost. This book will give God the glory because with him I know that all things are possible. And in Jesus' name, I declare healing and freedom on the lives of all those who read this book. So I celebrate in advance, because I know now that according to Romans 8:31, "If God is for us, who can be against us?"

I Am Woman

*"Usually when people are sad, they don't do anything.
They just cry over their condition. But when they get
angry, they bring about a change." Malcolm X*

Women being abused has been going on for years and years. From women being used for sex by their slave masters, to women having sex with their husbands when they didn't want to because of their "duty" as a wife. From women not having equal opportunities in the workforce, to women being unable to vote, the list can go on and on. I am proud to see we are living in a progressive generation. Everything may not be exactly where we would like, but we must think about how far we have come. Women are stepping up and challenging laws and society for equal treatment, opportunities, and safety. Women are no longer sitting around looking pretty and being quiet. We are roaring. We are marching. We are calling out all abusers. We are saying NO.

We live in a time where women are coming forward about their assaults and the mistreatments that they have experienced and have been experiencing. We see it every day, some CEO of some large corporation being charged with sexual assault or harassment. Laws are changing so women are safe in the workplace and in the real world. Arrests are being made. Lawsuits are being filed. We have so much information regarding rape culture. We are educating our society. We are putting an end to this. We as women have suffered long enough. Women are taking back their power. This fight has encouraged me to take back mine and to join the women who are fighting for our rights. I, just as the other women I see in the public eye, am making the sacrifice and coming forward and speaking on this unfair system and societal norms. We don't care about being liked, but doing what we believe is right. We're going against the normal societal expectations where women are supposed to be meek and unheard, instead of the powerful individuals we really are. I feel that as a young black woman it is my duty to let women of color know that they matter and they are valuable. They deserve to be seen and heard. They deserve to be felt. I am a human being and my feelings and respect should be honored. I don't have to do anything I do not want to do, especially if it compromises my integrity. I feel the shift happening in our culture today. I am proud to say that I am in awe and blessed to be able to witness this history. Women exerting their power should not make the men in our society feel less than or insecure. It should encourage men to rise up and fight alongside women, to meet women because each and every man was birthed by a woman. I have a duty to teach my son that women are valuable. They are to be treated with respect and kindness. And under no circumstance will it ever be ok to treat a woman less than humane.

Since I was a little girl, I can remember hearing the music of what he calls himself "pied-piper of R&B" R. Kelly. I grew up listening to his music and watching his videos. There have always been allegations of this man sleeping with underage women. It was something we all knew about but no one had the courage to do anything about it because he was for black people and our community. He was successful and a major league entertainer of his time. It was as if the black community let him slide because of his success. He sold his soul while making millions off of us and we cheered him on while he did it. Now present day women who he abused are finally getting the justice that they have for years been dying for. We live in a time where media is everything and news spreads very fast. I've recently seen R. Kelly arrested for aggravated sexual abuse, involving four females, three of whom were minors. In response to his arrest, he plead not guilty to all counts of the aggravated sexual abuse. These women have done their part. They have shared their stories. What we can do is sit and let God do his work. You will reap what you sow, and God always has the final say. It doesn't matter how much money you have. I believe justice will be served. To all the parties who were hurt, I send nothing but love, light, and healing their way. As previously stated, I know what it is like to be violated. That shame lives with you for a very long time. I am proud of these women coming forward and sharing so that the shame is released, putting the shame on display that they have been suffering though in silence for many years. These women are freeing themselves. They can now let their shame rest easily. Some people say these women deserved what they got because they were seeking fame. That is something that we may never know. But what we do know is that they did in fact get the fame they may have desired. They will be known in history for having the courage to share their stories. You see how God works. He always makes sure your troubles and pain are turned to good for his glory. These women may not even be aware of how many women they have freed by freeing themselves.

Black Girl Goals

As a kid, my grandmother and mother were always very honest and transparent with me about the struggles that they each have faced being dark skinned women. My grandmother would explain how growing up she was always bullied for having dark skin and how she developed self hatred because of it. She would always tell me I had the best complexion. I was right in the middle, not too dark and not too light. I didn't always love my brown skin. Although my skin complexion was in the middle, I still experienced discrimination, prejudice, and racism for being black period.

Growing up in the suburbs of Windsor, I experienced firsthand how being a black kid and not being surrounded by others who looked like me played a role in how I viewed myself. Most of my classes were honors classes in high school. There were a few of us in these classes but we weren't the majority. When I say we, I'm speaking for the black kids who weren't hiding their blackness so they could fit in. See I wasn't raised in the hood. My mother was able to get me out before I was old enough to remember, but my family was from the hood so naturally the hood was in me. I was often given that ghetto girl label, and I guess in a way I had all the behaviors that society told me were invaluable so I didn't care about the way I was portrayed. According to the world, I was already counted out. I was promiscuous, I shoplifted, and I had a real problem with authority.

I remember in the beginning of my history class while taking attendance, the teacher would call my name, and everyday he purposely mispronounced it. The first few times, I took it as an honest mistake because my name isn't common. As it continued, I began to feel that he was making a mockery out of me. I was the only black girl in the class. This experience contributed to my low self esteem. I began to look at my name as if it was ghetto. The shame of my name led me to internalize more feelings of low self worth.

My junior year, I had a professor for English; she was an older white woman, and very much utilized her power and privilege. At the beginning of each class, she would put a question on the board related to all kinds of life scenarios. Then after a few minutes of responding to the question, we were able to share our responses to the question as a collective.

One day, this question had to do with a mother who was addicted to drugs who lost her child to the system and wanted to get her kid back after getting clean—should she be given her child back? This response was easy for me being that I lived this. I wasn't given up to the system, however, I was familiar with having a parent who at one point was addicted to drugs.

My response was the woman should most definitely get her child back. Her response to my response was, and I'll never forget it, "so you're telling me that a crack head who gave birth to her child and finally got clean is deserving of getting her child back after losing them to the system." She made me feel like a fool. She made me feel worse about myself because of what that said to me, a little girl who had a parent who was a recovering addict. It feeds the narrative that black children or their parents are not valuable. I had a mother who was a recovering addict and a father in upstate New York doing federal time in prison. My teacher, a woman who had the ability to speak life into me, chose not to, instead she chose to categorize me with the rest of the kids who were considered "written off" in her book. That hurt.

As a parent it is so important to me for my son to know who he is. He is a black man and child of God. He is a king. There is royalty running through his blood. But the reality is one day he's going to go out in the world and be treated less than because of the color of his skin. When my son goes out into the world and the world tries to tell him who he is not, he will face the world and tell them who he is. Confidence and positive identity is crucial. I believe it is imperative that brown skin babies know how valuable they are early on. I don't want my son to have the same experiences that I had if and when he begins his education. So I choose to be proactive rather than reactive. I educate him and show him how beautiful his blackness is, how powerful he is, how smart he is by constantly giving him praise and recognition. Although he is only two, I talk to him, teaching him who God is and with God in his life there is nothing that he can't do.

Today, I am proud of the woman that I am. I am proud of my skin color. I walk in my power. I allow God's light to shine through me. I am blessed. I am light. I lack nothing.

Nothing Real Can Be Threatened

Marriane Williamson's *A Return to Love*, one of my very favorite books, was created on her reflections of a Course in Miracles, which states there is no such thing as hate. Only love exists, and the opposite of love is not hate, but fear. When I watch my son interact and play I look at him in awe. He is truly fearless. He tests limits and objects anything that he doesn't feel is right for him. As parents, it is our job to guide our children and teach them, while also creating a safe space so they could grow into the adults that God has created them to be. But lately I feel as if I have learned so much through him. He doesn't care who is watching, or who is around. He just does and just is. He moves to the beat of his own drum. I look at this behavior and then look at the behavior of adults including myself. We rarely take risks, and often only do things we know we are capable of doing. We seek comfort in things we know and of which are sure. Where along the journey did we lose that fearlessness?

Our first experiences are shaped from childhood. Somewhere during our first experiences we may have tried to do something or told our parents something we liked and they shut us down or discouraged us, leaving us feeling insecure and fearful. We may have experienced rejection in school by our classmates or teachers, sometimes even the people we considered our friends. Childhood is crucial for receiving unconditional love and nurturing. We need validation from our loved ones so we aren't going out in the world looking for it as adults, instead of using people, material things, drugs, or success as a way of measuring our self worth, know that you are already worthy.

You are worthy just because you were born. God loves us so much and already deems us qualified just because we are a part of him and we were created in his image. When I began to seek a deeper relationship with God and read his word, it was then that I really knew just how much he loved me and how valuable I was. My whole adult life I had been living in fear and not living my life according to who God called me to be. I was insecure, I was doubtful, and I didn't believe in myself or him. I didn't see myself through God's eyes because I really didn't know who he was and who I was. As my relationship with God became more intimate, so did the relationship I had with myself. I started to view myself the way God views me. In response, my life began to change. I began to say no to things, people, and places that did not serve me. I ended relationships and friendships that I was pouring into without reciprocity. I began to walk, talk, and act more confident in myself. I began to live my life boldly and loud. God created us to shine. He created us to live a life of abundance. We all have God's love and power flowing through us; we just have to be open to receive. We can't continue to live in fear. Living in fear keeps us from not only blessings that God has in store for us, but the purpose he has for our lives. We all have a purpose and a duty that God wants each and every one of us to fulfill. When we feel afraid, the most we must know that God is always with us, guiding us and protecting us. We don't have to rely on ourselves or carry all of our worries and burdens. We just have to be able to trust and surrender.

Have you ever felt that restless feeling? Like you are accomplishing things in life but you still feel as if something is missing. You may have a good job and a family, a career, a house, education, a beautiful face and body but still feel a void inside of you. That void is something that only God can fill up. We are all yearning and seeking something, and that something is the unconditional love from God. I did not feel content until I began to fill myself up with God's love. Even when I thought I was happy it never lasted long. I used temporary things to fill me up. Sometimes it was men and sex, sometimes alcohol and weed, other times it was partying and going out. Mainly I used success and being busy as a way to cope with the life I hated. I graduated nursing school at the age of 22. I lived on my own. I was what you called an independent woman, and nobody could tell me nothing because on paper I had everything I ever wanted. Sometimes you don't know how empty you really are until you accomplish all the things you have wanted, and then you realize you are still unhappy. No tangible thing can make up for the love and belonging each one of us desire.

I know my story may not resonate with everyone, but to the people that my story does resonate with, if you don't remember anything I say, I want you to know how much God loves you. He loves you so much, and no matter what you have been through, God will still use you. You have purpose and you matter. God is depending on you to embrace your purpose so you can help him fulfill his divine plan that each and every one of us plays a major role in. No matter how small it may be, God will use you through your gifts and talents. He will use you through your jobs, your friends, and your family. Someone is waiting for you to step into your purpose so you can enlighten them to step into their own. We all are on this road together. If you are a believer and you love God, I want you to know that everything you are, has, is and want will be used for his good. He has the power to turn it all around. When God is for you, nothing can be against you. Don't think about how hard it will be. Do it anyway. Don't think about what your friends and family will say. It's going to be more difficult for you to accept living a life you don't want rather than stepping out on faith. The suffering you already feel can't get any worse than that, and the longing for joy and fulfillment and happiness will never go away. So what do you have to lose?

Sitting here writing this book, it took me years and years to get here. I knew I wanted to be a writer. I knew I wanted to help and reach masses of people through the telling of my story. I knew I wanted to share with people that you don't have to suffer. You don't have to live a life that is not fulfilling. I had to give my own self permission. I was the one holding me back. I knew what God promised me. I couldn't think about what my friends would say or my family. I had to do what would glorify God. That was to share my testimony. Don't let your current or past situations make you think that your talents and gifts can not be used. Everything about you, God created for a reason. Everything. From your style, to the way you talk, the way you dress, the values you believe in, what you are passionate about. None of that is by accident.

Faith Over Fear

One of the ways that I held myself back was, I used to think that it was too soon for me to try to help people. I convinced myself that I still needed more time healing and developing. I still needed more education to qualify for what God already said was mine. Who are you to talk about God and a testimony? I didn't grow up in a church. I always thought that only people who were from a Church were qualified to talk about God. I'm a random girl from a small town who heard God's call and answered. I pushed the path despite what the naysayers had to say. I had to remember what God said. God is for everybody. He loves each and everyone of us.

I used to want people to think that I had it all together. Now I don't care what people think. I want you to know that I was a mess and God turned my mess, everything that I have been through, into a message. He used my pain for purpose. He used my pain to push me, to motivate me, to encourage me to get to work. He made me so uncomfortable, I had no choice but to move. For years I was waiting for God to come and get me. The truth of the matter is, I didn't really have all the faith that

I thought I did. I have been aware of my purpose and gifts for a very long time. I have been aware of the promises that God made. Yet I was still stuck. Still not moving. Fear still had me paralyzed. And if I truly had faith in God, why would I still be afraid? Rationally that didn't make sense to me. I know that God is always here with me. I know he cleared the path for me. I know that nothing can be against me because God is for me. So why was I allowing fear to keep me stuck? I tried everything. I prayed, fasted, and lived in my bible. Nothing erased the fear that I had in my heart, but doing. Exercising my faith was going to be the only way I was able to truly witness the miracle of God. Faith without works is dead. So one day, I took the leap. I silenced the negative thoughts that were going through my mind. I haven't been saved long enough. God said do it anyway. But I'm not the perfect Christian and I'm still learning. God said do it anyway. I'm still struggling with doubt, fear and shame. God said do it anyway. "But" is an excuse that the enemy will try to use. It shows that you have doubt, and any chance of doubt is an opportunity to take over your thoughts and quit before you even begin. He doesn't want you to shine your light and magnify God's name. He wants you to be with a spouse who mistreats you, to stay at a job you hate, to stay stuck in whatever rut you may feel that you are in. The enemy wants to keep you in bondage. The enemy's objective is to rob, kill, and destroy. Don't let the enemy win.

I didn't want to wake up anymore and go to a job that I just like. I want to do what God purposed me for every day and all day. I want to wake up and not even feel like I'm going to work. I don't want to thank God that it's Friday. I want to thank God for every day. For giving me a vision. To believe that I could make another way. I want to live a life of empowerment, courage, joy, happiness and abundance. I don't want to struggle. I know you don't want to struggle. You can do all things through Christ who strengthens you.

Daddy Issues

My father has been out of my life more than I can remember him being in my life. He has been in and out of jail since I was born. The lack of love and presence from a parent or caregiver plays such a major role in your life. When a child does not receive the love and care that they need, that doesn't mean that the child's needs go away. The child will usually just go elsewhere to fill the void, which is the route that I took.

I never really developed an emotional attachment to my father. How could I if I never established trust with him that is critical for a child to develop healthy attachment? I never really knew I was masking the hurt of an absent father in my life until I became a mother. Becoming a mother changed and put so many things into a new perspective for me. I love my son with my entire being, he's the reason I wake up every morning. He's the reason why I strive to be a healed, whole individual. He's influenced so many things in my life since the moment I found out I was blessed with a child. So when I think about my father and him having the choice of being in my life and not choosing to be there, it bothers me—to be honest it hurts me.

My father's longest bid was from the time I was nine years old until I was about twenty. Throughout his time in prison, he was pretty consistent in my life. We spoke often. We would spend as much time as his call time would allow. I felt like our relationship was open and honest. I can think back and hear so vividly my dad's boisterous laugh. My dad is really a clown. He loves to crack jokes. Most of our phone time was spent talking about life and him making jokes about everything. He did his bid in federal prison in upstate New York, close to Canada. My mom brought me up there one time. It was beautiful. The snow on the mountains in the springtime, I can still see it fresh in my mind. I just knew when my dad came home from prison I was finally going to get my daddy back, and we would be able to make up for lost time. I would finally be able to be the daddy's girl I had always dreamed about being. Unfortunately, that time never came and eight years after him being released from prison, I finally stopped waiting on it to happen. I've accepted that my father may never be able to be the father that the little girl inside of me needs him to be. I've accepted that my father doesn't have the tools to give me the little girl fairy tale that is still embedded in my imagination. But that doesn't change or take away the feeling of loss that I still feel inside, the pain that I still feel, or the void that I feel when those moments come up that I need a dad for and I don't have one.

I think the reason why I never made a big deal about the fact that my father was in prison is because through those walls we both were still able to maintain our relationship. I felt his effort even hundreds of miles away. When my father was first released from prison I was so excited. I visited him in the halfway house. I just wanted to be around him. I just wanted to jump in his arms and have him spin me around and around. Those moments never came.

Once my dad left the halfway house, he was able to move back with my step mother who has been in my life since before I could remember. I believe I have a closer relationship with her than my own father. When my father was in jail, my step mother and my mother made sure that I was able to visit and spend time with my younger brother. If there were ever personal feelings between my mother and step mother, I was never aware of it.

My mother had moved on and gotten married to my step father who also had children from a previous relationship. My mother raised her step children as if they came from her own body. She treated us all equal

QUANIECE RAQUELLE

and loved us all. There was never a situation where I was being treated better because I was her kid. The same for my step mother. She never made me feel like I didn't belong. I often went to visit her. When I saw her around while my father was locked up she would hug me and cry and tell me how much she loved me and how much I looked just like my father. That lady treated me with so much love and I will forever have the utmost respect for her.

When my father was released from prison one thing I can say, he did the right thing, and really got himself together and didn't go back. As the years went on after being released, we would keep in contact with each other. He came to my 21st birthday party, my nursing school graduation, and my baby shower. The major things that went on in my life, he made the effort to be involved. We'd have calls on holidays and birthdays. I would go see him on father's day, but the intimate emotional bond that I was expecting to get never came. I gave it time. I reached out. I was patient. I didn't really have experience asking for what I needed so I never told him I wanted to have a closer relationship; I just assumed as my father he would know that that was what I needed. It's what every little girl needs. And although I was a woman in a woman body, the little girl inside of me still longed for my daddy's love.

When I became a mother, my outlook on parenting totally changed. I reflected on my childhood a lot. I took what I wanted and left a lot behind. I didn't want to raise my son the way that I had been raised. I wanted to raise my son with love and emotional support and nurturing so that he wouldn't be out in the world looking for it. I want my son to know who he is in Christ and who he belongs to. He is God's creation. Identity can only be found in the person who created you. Not your mother or your father, peers, co-workers and friends. When you are aware of who you are you have the internal power to say no to everything that is not for you. You won't be influenced by others. You won't be living the life someone else wants you to live.

I try my best to be mindful of the way that I pour into my son. My son has a purpose that God intended for his life, and I never want to intercede. My job as his mother is to love him and guide him in the right direction, and the best way that I can do that is by being an example to him. By loving God and showing him who God is, I have faith that one day he will grow and develop his own relationship with God. On those days that he is unsure and filled with doubt, he will know who he can call on to seek wisdom. On those days when loneliness creeps in, he will know that he is never alone, that God is always with him, and by keeping God first he could trust that everything will always work out for his good.

The pain that I felt from the strained relationship I had with my father began to fester, and when I gave birth to my son that hurt transformed to anger. Emotionally, I was experiencing everything. Every feeling that I had suppressed began to manifest. All the emotions and pain that I had been hiding hit me like a ton of bricks, literally. I became angry, angry for all the years I waited for him in jail, and even more angry for the years I waited for him after he came home. I was tired of waiting. I was overwhelmed and I felt like I was in a cage suffocating in emotions and thoughts.

I assumed that because my father wasn't really a good father to me, he would step up and be a better grandparent to my son, his first grandchild. That never came. As my son grew and the lack of my father's presence grew, so did my anger. I had tried to be there for my father, and I made it fairly easy for him to be there for me, and I still couldn't understand why the relationship wasn't how I felt it should be. I could take him not being there for me; I was able to excuse that. But not being there for my son and not loving my son? I took that very personally. It infuriated me. Any respect I had for him was lost. I shut him out.

For years I used the excuse of him not knowing how to be a parent because he was raised without his own father. I now know that isn't an excuse. I see amazing fathers who didn't have fathers, not only love their children, but wanted to be very hands on. I've seen fathers who had failed relationships with their child's mother and still would not let that stop them from being present in raising their child. It's hard for me to say that my father doesn't know how to be a father when I see him being a father to my two younger brothers and my step sisters. He had my youngest brother with my step mom after coming home from prison. I loved my siblings very much but I can't lie and say that I wasn't filled with jealousy. I was jealous because I never got to have my father all to myself. It was always as if I had to come second to whatever else was going on. I don't even think I've ever sat down and ate a meal with just my father and I. As a grown woman who has been living on my own, my father has never even come to my house to visit me, to fix something, or to kill a few spiders. I invited him. He never showed up.

One day at work while talking to a coworker and telling her about the relationship I had with my father, she gave me some advice and that was to pray. After trying everything myself, the one thing I never did was pray about it. Prayer changes things, and when you pray about it God hears you. He hears each and every one of your prayers. I didn't immediately pray for God to reconcile the relationship with my father, pride was holding me back. I felt like it was his responsibility to mend our broken relationship. I also felt like if I admitted to God that I wanted him to fix it, I would first have to acknowledge that I still wanted a relationship with my father after him hurting me. That was a very hard pill to swallow, and I knew that I had to give myself some time. I knew that one day I would say that prayer. I still needed God to continue working in me.

The issues that I had with my father began to affect the relationship I had with my son's father. I began to lash out on him anytime he made a mistake having to do with our son. I was projecting the pain I felt onto him.

I don't enjoy being angry but it was part of my process and I allow myself to feel all that I am feeling. The overwhelming anger that was brewing on the inside of me is what finally led me to pray. I prayed and asked God to reconcile my family. I asked God to heal the broken relationship that I had with my father. I asked God to heal my family period. I prayed and prayed for my family's healing. I was honest with God about my desires and for the first time in my life I admitted to God and myself that I really wanted my dad to be a part of my life. I wanted to let go of the past. I had to get to the root of my anger to uncover what I really desired inside of my heart. A part of loving yourself is being honest with yourself. The truth was I still wanted to have a relationship with my father. So I finally prayed and surrendered. My father on Earth may never be what I want him to be. I know now that I do have a father in Heaven and his love is unchanging and doesn't waver. I am a child of God.

You Can't Pour From an Empty Vessel

When you depend on others to fill you up with love where there is a void, they have the ability to take it away with them when and if they shall ever leave. People have the right to change their mind at any given time. The reality of people is that we are all human. Underneath our titles, positions, and high places that we may be in life, at the end of it all we are all still just human. We will fail. We will hurt others. We will experience emotions. Even the emotions that we aren't always proud of or don't give ourselves permission to feel such as anger, shame, doubt and fear. These feelings will always be a part of us because we are having a human experience here on Earth. This is why we must always be dependent upon him. God's love is unchanging. Nothing you do will ever be able to separate you from his love. That is why you must put all your worries and fears onto him. He will never turn his back on you. As humans on Earth, we will constantly be in a battle of our flesh. God is a jealous God. He wants you to need him. He wants you to call on him when you need help. Do not feel guilty for turning to God when you are suffering. God is a healer and a provider and he will provide and heal you within every area of your life. That is the power of God.

Life can make us change. Loving God and living for him will make you change, in areas you never thought were possible. From my experience, I believe that life hardens us. It puts us in survival mode. We can't be who we really are because we are too busy trying to survive. With loving God, I find myself not becoming but "unbecoming;" unbecoming everything I thought I had to be in order to survive. I now know that me being provided for comes from God. He always makes sure I am never without. No longer am I operating in survival mode. I rely on God to take care of me and fight my battles. I can focus on what he wants me to focus on— HIM.

When you are whole, the lack of love from outside sources doesn't take away because you are already full, and you've been filled by God, and God's well will quench your thirst for life. When you are full, you know what you bring to the table. You know the value that you have. When or if a person chooses to walk away you know that them walking away really doesn't have anything to do with you or your worth. God protects us and he does that by closing doors. Yet, we tend to still stare at that door after he has closed it, questioning why. He has something better for you, something greater. He has something he designed just for you.

Think of yourself as a cup. In that cup you are filled with fluid. The fluid is the self-love. You get your fluid from the source which is God. When that cup is filled by God it never runs out. In fact, your cup will run over. When your cup is halfway full or sometimes even empty, you will look to fill that cup back up. Where we go wrong is we don't go back to the original source for the refill. We seek titles, positions, wealth, relationships and material possessions to make us feel better, and we never do so we think we need more. I'm gonna call it "love thirsty." When you are love thirsty, any kind of fluid that fills you up feels good, even if it's not good for you. That's why it's so important to make sure your cup is filled by God because it's the perfect love. God's love fills you up in a way that nothing else can compare. God's love makes you see yourself the way he sees you. He created us to desire love and belonging so don't ever feel guilty for wanting to fulfill those desires. The problem is most of the time we don't involve him in the equation when we are presented with certain people and things. We are so eager to just be full, we justify those red flags. We justify the wrong that feels so right. The truth is you have value just because of the fact that you are breathing. If you woke up this morning, you have value. Why? Because you still have a purpose that God wants you to fulfill. If you are still alive there is something that God wants to do through you. You still have an assignment that God needs you to fulfill for his greater good. He did not create you to be in anything mediocre. God wants you to live an abundant life, not only just after you die in heaven but also on Earth. He wants you to show the world how he has blessed you. Not so others can be jealous, but so they can know that if God does it for you he can do it for them too. He wants you to show the world what can happen if you just depend on him and have faith that he will provide and be with you to the very end.

My life is bigger than just my relationships and career. Yes, they are a part of my experiences and they have shaped me, but this path is a journey—a journey back home. We are all learning, growing, and experiencing life every single day. Every interaction, every relationship or friendship, is all for a bigger purpose.

We are all connected

Now that you have gotten a little background information on how I was raised and where I come from, I would like to explain why I feel that self-love, and the importance of not just having it but believing and implementing it, is so important. I've been through some very hard times in my life. Most of the time, I got myself into these situations. With God, I have overcome every single one. I've had major low points as well as major comebacks. Every lesson. Every mistake. Every friendship. Every relationship. Every struggle. Every tear I cried from the loneliness I felt was all worth it. It all led me to God, where I belong. For the first time in my life, I finally feel like I belong.

During those hard times in my life, I often found myself feeling alone, like no one else in the entire world could be going through the same things I have gone through. Boy, was I wrong. Each and every one of us is a lot more alike than we would like to admit. God connected us all. One of us suffers, we all suffer. When one of us wins, we all win. Although we live in a society that values individualism, each of our own individual choices and values affect us all as a whole. That is why our world as a whole is suffering.

I used to think that I was the only person who had insecurities and abandonment issues, toxic family issues and generational curses. I felt that I was the only person that stayed in a toxic relationship longer than I should have, and gave away pieces of myself to others who were undeserving. Or that I was the only woman who had a child out of wedlock, or been involved in a love triangle. I felt like no one could possibly understand all the pain that I was going through, so I kept most of the pain to myself, killing myself in the process. I felt like I was literally dying at a point in my life.

When I was keeping that pain to myself, I dove into research. I've always naturally been a reader. Reading is how I learn. Reading is a part of who I am— a student. I began to research about love, relationships, and self-love. I read every book I could, took courses, watched videos. I used any way that I could gain information on this phenomenon of self love that I didn't know much about. Over the years I began to study the people around me. I began to see patterns amongst the people around me. As I learned more, I began to gain clarity. I felt like the light bulb had gone off. Biologically our brains are programmed to search for a solution even without us consciously trying to do so. Our mind is so powerful.

Although each and every one of us all have our own individual experiences, our desires and needs aren't that much different. We feel the need to be loved and accepted, and to feel like you belong. I know this because I searched for that feeling my entire life. On that search, I kept coming to the conclusion that as much as we seek that feeling and project it onto external things, it will never work. That emptiness that we project onto our jobs, relationships, children, and family members will never fulfill the love we have to give to ourselves that we receive from God.

Scientifically, it has been proven that babies will not survive without love and attachment from a caregiver. Many hospitals have volunteers who come to the hospital just to hold sick infants in the NICU so that their health can turn around. We need love. We need to feel connected, yet not at the expense of losing yourself and your soul.

So how do we change our thoughts and habits from what we have been socialized to believe is right and normal? Especially being a woman. It's ingrained in us to put other's needs and wants before our own. As a social work major, I can recall being in one of my classes and my professor did a survey. The survey wasn't fancy, she simply just asked each of us to raise our hand. The question was, "Do you fear that having children could get in the way of your success?" As I looked around the classroom, knowing I had a one year old at home that I felt so guilty about leaving to pursue my education, I was so shocked. Not one man's hand was raised in the classroom. Only women. All the women feared that it would come a time where they would have to put their careers that they loved and worked so hard to get on the back burner, to have and raise a family. Yet here I was living it. I am a single parent, going to school full-time. I am the CEO of my home, as well as having to work at my day job. But God's provided me with the strength to do it all. I am the exception to the rule. Some days I have no idea how it gets done. I just rely on God to get me through. I know it sounds so hard to do, but doing something so simple as relying on God can relieve the heaviness that you are carrying, when you don't have to. God wants to carry it for you. He will carry it for you. But you have to ask. Isaiah 40:31 says, "But those who hope in the LORD will renew their strength. They will soar on wings like eagles; they will run and not grow weary, they will walk and not be faint."

Now don't get me wrong, being a parent means you have to make a lot of sacrifices. You naturally want to put your children's needs before your own, burning yourself out in the process. But how can you be a healthy parent and partner if you are suffering? How can you tend to your partner's or children's needs if you haven't tended to your own? As women, I find that we have a hard time with asking for help, especially in the black community. We have to be a superwoman no matter what and if we even look like we need help, we will die from humiliation. It's as if when we aren't running on E, we are doing something wrong. I'm here to break that curse. Not only in my own family, but by writing this book I hope to bring some answers to questions you may have never considered.

After having my son, I found it extremely hard to transition back to work. Every woman is not the same. I've met some mothers who couldn't wait to get back to work. Being in the house drove them insane. But to the mothers who don't feel that way, it's ok. It's ok to miss your babies and to want to love on them, and co-sleep with them. I've learned in the beauty of parenthood that how you raise your children and interact with them is catered to your own individual preferences. You don't have to raise your children the way you have seen the women before you. You also don't have to shame other mothers for deciding to do something differently than you. Different things work for different individuals.

I had a very good idea of the kind of parent I wanted to be. And before that, I had a very good idea of the kind of woman I wanted to be. But experiences change you. They change your perspective. They change your mind. I am not the same woman that I was before I found out that I was pregnant. I am not the same woman that I was yesterday. God's power has the ability to change you every single day.

Therapy for a Black Girl

When I had my son I suffered from postpartum depression, and I was lashing out on the ones closest to me. Resentment from my own childhood began to bubble up to the surface. Things weren't going how I wanted them to with my child's father. I was a total emotional wreck. I was on my way to a mental breakdown. I felt like I hadn't done anything for me in such a long time. Not to mention mourning the loss of my own self before becoming a mother. I was really struggling and didn't know what would help me. I decided to go back to therapy. I needed an outlet. I needed to talk to someone who wouldn't have judgment on me like in my personal life.

That wasn't my first experience going into therapy. Over the years, I had been in and out of therapy several times, going back usually when something major or traumatic had happened, but never finding someone I truly connected with to dig deeper. I needed to find a therapist that I could really connect with. When I did find her, it was as if God sent her directly here for me. So much that she is one of the reasons that influenced me to go back to school and get a degree in social work. Sitting on that couch, me, her, and God, we were able to slowly but surely piece my life back together. Through therapy, I was able to sort through many unresolved childhood issues that I had been battling with subconsciously.

When you invite God into those areas you are struggling in, he has the ability to turn it all around. I also learned that it was ok to be selfish. Selfish? Somebody reading this probably has a red flag going off in their heads right now. But, "I said what I said" in my best Nene Leakes voice. It's most certainly okay to be selfish, to do what you need to do to honor yourself and God. That doesn't mean going around mistreating people to cater to your own needs but to set boundaries and ask for help when you need it, to honor those feelings that you feel that you may not be proud of.

As a new mother, I felt so bad for saying I needed a break. That I couldn't take it anymore and that I was on the verge of snapping. But the guilt that I felt from feeling that was eating me alive. How could anyone need a break from their child? The truth was I needed a break from my life. Mourning the loss of myself while adjusting with a new child alone was one of the hardest seasons of my life. I'm what you call a recovering perfectionist. I had to do everything right and do it with perfection in order to feel worthy. I was failing motherhood with flying colors, so I thought. I felt horrible about it.

Going to therapy taught me to be gentle and patient with myself, to talk to myself with love and care. The way that I was talking to myself was horrible, which in turn reflected why I felt the way that I felt. You have to meet yourself and honor yourself wherever you are in the process. Honor those ugly feelings just as much as you honor the pretty ones. Love yourself regardless of what you are accomplishing, love yourself just for being who God created you to be. When you were born, you weren't born with a title, a degree, a car, a house, or a partner. You were born because God had a plan. He knew you before you even walked this earth. He loved you before you were ever conceived in your mother's womb. And you didn't have to do anything to receive that love but just be you, whoever that might be.

I want not only women to know but men as well, that loving yourself is normal and it is critical. Self-love is so important that I decided to dedicate my life to it.

My career path initially started off with me working as a nurse, hence the caregiver role. But I realized I didn't really enjoy taking care of people. It was actually kind of exhausting. I burnt out very fast after my first couple of years in the nursing field. So, I decided to take some time off from furthering my education until I was sure of my next steps. I took a couple of years to just study life and love and experience. I developed hobbies and passions. During that time, I gained several certifications and took several love, life, and spiritual courses. Mostly things that I thought I didn't need or would ever use, but my desire to know and learn was very strong.

During that time off, I knew that I wanted to go back to school, but I was still unsure of what. I wanted this next pursuit to be aligned with who I am now, and still be able to provide the space where I can grow with this career. I thought what could I do in my career where I taught people how to love and care for themselves? I know that I'm good at listening to others and allowing others to feel seen and heard without judgment. I know that I am a mother now and I wanted a flexible schedule to be able to be there for my son.

God already created me to be a counselor. It's what I already did in my real life. Why not make a career out of it? Then as I began to learn more, and actually get the intellectual education in addition to applying my life experiences, it was almost as if everything seemed to just fall right into place. Even when I got off track I was still on track, because God uses everything for his good and his glory. The good, the bad, and the ugly.

Talk to Me Nice

I can truly say one of the most important things I have learned on my journey to self-love, is being gentle with yourself. We so often get caught up giving, and being kind to others around us and forget to love on and be kind to ourselves. Have you ever really sat down and thought about all the negative things we say to ourselves throughout our day? We really aren't nice to ourselves if you think about it.

But how can you be nice to yourself when you really don't like who you are? You don't like the things you have done or the experiences of pain that have shaped you to be the person that you are. We are our own worst enemy. Why? Because we spend the most time with ourselves in our own head.

Imagine the time and progress and amazing things we could do and accomplish if we directed that negative self-talk to positive self-talk. Instead of beating ourselves up for what we didn't know or do but instead think of ourselves as learning, and progressing and doing the best we can.

One of my favorite teachers is Iyanla Vanzant. I've learned so much about myself from utilizing her workbooks, self-help books, and Youtube videos. Iyanla often says, "people love you the best way they know how at that time." That resonated with me and I believe that that goes for loving yourself as well.

If we all knew how to love ourselves correctly, wouldn't we be doing it? As I look around, more and more people are working towards healing. Healing those wounds that tell us we are unworthy. Healing those wounds that keep us living in shame. Those wounds that keep us from living a life of abundance and happiness.

Many of us are not willing to do the work. Self-love looks cute, pretty, and shiny on the outside. But it is some of the hardest, darkest, time-consuming work I have ever done in my life. So I've learned to be gentle with myself and take it day by day. Take the lessons as they come. Live life as it comes. Every trial, every tribulation, every tear you cry is for a greater purpose. Just because you didn't do as well as you thought you did does not make you a failure. You are still living. You have the ability to live and fight another day as long as you don't give up.

Giving up is not an option. You can stop, you can cry, you can pause. But you must not throw in the towel. You are worth it and your life is worth living. You are worth the fight. Be gentle with yourself. Be kind to you. Be patient with you. You are in this body for your whole life. Get to know it. Get to know God and who he created you to be.

God's Plan

From a very young age, I was very aware of my feelings. Growing up, I thought something was wrong with me because I was very sensitive. I used to cry about a lot of things, ok I'm going to be real my sensitive behind used to cry about everything. Harsh words hurt, they still do. I realized that the reason for this is because my love language is words of affirmation. Our love language is often what we didn't receive in our childhood.

But life has happened and with a lot of self-work, I developed a strong sense of self and I have realized that most of what people project onto you, actually has nothing to do with you but more about them. People project.

In my younger years, I was bullied. I was quiet and kind, and I didn't like confrontation, I also didn't like when people got into fights around me. From early on I knew I didn't like drama and tried to stay far away from it. I guess that made me a target for being picked on. Plus, putting myself out there to make friends wasn't an option. I have always been very aware and knew who and what I wanted to be around.

Books were my safe place. My mother made sure I spent a lot of time in the library and in bookstores. Because of that background, I believe I developed a love for reading stories, which transitioned to my love of writing. Journaling is something I've been doing my whole life. I didn't really have anyone to talk to, so I wrote it all down. Everything. I still have my childhood journals to this day. My first journal had a little lock on it that came with a tiny little key.

Judy Blume's *"Are You There God? It's Me, Margaret"* was one of the first chapter books that I had read and my favorite book at that. Not even realizing that this little girl was talking to God on a regular basis. Sharing her deepest darkest secrets with him, not being ashamed about anything. That book was also written in a different time, when talking about God and religion in social settings wasn't as taboo or offensive as it is now. When I think about that book, it was centered around God and different religions, as well as family and its dynamic. Everything that I am passionate about.

It's so crazy because as a child we always get asked what do you want to be when you grow up and I never ever considered being a writer, even though I loved to write and tell stories. I loved to tell my stories. I knew that I was compassionate and wanted to help others, I just wasn't sure in which way. I knew who God was and I knew that I was supposed to love him, but I never developed a personal relationship with him until my early adult years. I don't regret that time that I didn't know him because through that time he knew me. He created me. He loved me. He was only waiting for me to seek him, and then he appeared. It was through my hard times that I did finally seek him when I knew that I couldn't go another day without his guidance and love.

The first time that I experienced the presence of God was when I was on my deathbed. Or, what I thought was my death bed because I am still here thank you, God. At nineteen, I got saved and professed my love for Jesus Christ. I professed that he died for me so that I could live. Two weeks later I got into a car accident.

The car accident didn't put me in the hospital, but the pain I experienced after did. Due to all the pain I was experiencing, I was given a muscle relaxer and pain pills. Now y'all know my experience with drugs and how I came from a family of addictions, there's no way I should have been taking any kind of narcotics. But I did. I was in too much pain to know otherwise.

After a few days of laying around in pain from the accident, I had to return to the scheduled program of my life. At the time I was in school. I was working full time, and it was a lot going on. So much going on that I didn't even have time to realize that my body was under attack.

The accident was the other driver's fault, she smashed into my car from behind. Afterward, I had to go see a lawyer and go to physical therapy. That specific day in therapy I recall being in extreme pain. I thought I was just having muscle spasms. I had already been to the hospital a second time after the accident and was told by the doctor that what I was experiencing was muscle spasms. So I just took the muscle relaxers or pain pills when I was in pain. I had taken my prescribed dose that day but nothing was working. I was still in excruciating pain. I figured I just needed to work out the kinks in my back and I had already had a physical therapy appointment scheduled, so I would wait until I got there.

While doing my physical therapy, my therapist mentioned that I was breathing at an extreme rate. He offered to take my vital signs. After taking them, he saw that my heart rate was extremely high and recommended that I go to the emergency room just down the street. I felt that I was capable of driving myself since it was right down the street, so I did.

When I arrived at the emergency room, after giving all my information and history and they took my own vital signs, they admitted me. I told my mom and loved ones, who came to the hospital to be with me. After receiving an x-ray, it was confirmed that I was suffering from pneumonia, and not only did I have pneumonia I had a blood clot that was lodged in my lung. This would explain all the pain in my back and why I was having such a hard time breathing.

I immediately became the patient for all the medical students to learn from. Every morning they would stand around my bedside and explain exactly what was going on with me. I had to go through several tests and blood draws, because they put me on heparin, a blood thinner, to clear up the clots in my lungs. They couldn't understand how a person so young could get blood clots.

At the time I had been on birth control, which increased my risk of clots. As well as laying in bed, which caused me to get pneumonia. All my tests were coming up negative for genetic blood disorders, they just couldn't figure it out. Still to this day I do not have an exact cause of why I had blood clots. But that history I always have to be mindful of, because when you have them once, it puts you at higher risk for receiving them again.

I spent seventeen days laid in a hospital bed. I was going crazy in there. During the day I got poked and probed with needles. In the evening, I could spend time with my family and loved ones because people had work and other obligations throughout the day.

This particular day I was having a visit from a family friend. We were just sitting talking about regular life stuff and out of nowhere I got this unbearable pain. The family friend called the doctors where they immediately tried to give me something for the spasms and pain through my IV. Nothing worked. They attempted to push pain medication for a second time with no change. Their response was to give it a little while to kick it your body is working extremely hard right now. With IV therapy being that the needle is already in the vein, you should feel immediate relief after receiving medication because it goes straight to the bloodstream. After minutes of moaning and groaning and still no relief, my family friend began to call out to Jesus and pray over me. Not only did she pray, but she also laid her hands on me. I don't remember much but what I do remember was within minutes, from the top of my head going all the way down my body, to the bottom of my feet the pain began to subside and I felt a sense of peace over my body.

If I didn't believe in the power of prayer before, from that moment on I became a believer. Prayer works, and when praises go up, blessings come down.

Luv Drought

After being released from the hospital, I began a relationship with my best friend. After countless irrelevant relationships, at that time I had finally felt like I found the one. The love I had for him went beyond just the typical boyfriend and girlfriend kind of love. He was my legit best friend. I held him to a very high pedestal. He came to visit me every day in the hospital and would sit with me sometimes just to watch me rest.

When I decided to get into this relationship I went into it holding nothing back. He already knew all my secrets and desires and we had been friends for years, so us transitioning our friendship to a romantic relationship had to be a piece of cake. Or so I thought. This relationship was life-changing for me. This relationship broke me. At the end of it all I lost not only the person I wanted to spend my life with but the best friend who was always there to help me pick up the pieces when my world crumbled. How do you cope when the one person who used to make it better was the one constantly hurting you?

Being in this relationship with my best friend was when I first began to experience feelings of shame. I didn't know then what the feeling was but I just know he went from looking at me like I was his favorite person on earth to the most disgusting person on earth, and it hurt me so much.

The first few months were wonderful. It went well. Because of him, I wanted to be a better person. I wanted to be a power couple and I wanted us to build an empire together. He became my project. I dove into making sure he was going to be the best man I needed him to be. I wanted him to be my husband and I wasn't going to just marry anybody.

I was in school for nursing so I felt like it was only right that he did the same thing. We did homework together, I took classes, and then when I would complete them I would save everything and give it to him so he could have a head start. I loved him and I wanted him to do well.

I was ambitious and had dreams and knew exactly what I wanted and I wanted him to want the same things as me. I was trying to control him and make him into who I wanted him to be, leaving him feeling insecure and less than even though that wasn't my goal. I was only doing what I had seen the women around me do; take my man and make him into the best thing he can be instead of allowing him to be his own person and still loving him while he found his own way.

While I was pushing him, he was pushing me away. I found out within six months of our relationship that he had been cheating on me with one of the girls from his past. I would soon learn there were several girls from his past that he cheated on me with.

I never thought to question him a whole lot or get a whole lot of information about his whereabouts. This was my first relationship. I thought he loved me just as much as I loved him, and there was no way he would jeopardize everything we were working so hard for. I remember seeing the red flags but ignoring them. Sometimes I would go on his computer and in the login on Facebook, that same girl's email used to already be in the login. I ignored that. I actually went to high school with her and knew her quite well. We were friends on Facebook. I was never the type to post my significant other all over my page so I never posted him, but I was very sure that people knew about us. Or so I thought.

I really can't remember when I first found out that he was still dealing with her. I had gone away for the weekend with my family. It was right after my 20th birthday. He had lost his job the day of my birthday so his mood and behavior had been a little off. I figured he was just going through the funk of losing a good job. I knew we were going to be okay in the long run because we had each other. I was going to be his rock through whatever. He was my best friend and I would never leave him when he was down.

When I returned from vacation, he was a completely different person. He was angry and irritable and was treating me like shit when on my birthday he had just bought me a promise ring.

She finally inboxed me on Facebook and when I read the messages it broke my heart. I confronted him and of course, he denied it. He actually avoided me and tried to flip it on me by throwing my ex-boyfriends in my face. He told me that I was probably still messing with all of the guys I messed with before we made it official. I couldn't believe that he would take it there. I would never hurt him. When he and I decided to make our relationship official, anyone from my past I cut off. I didn't need to keep in contact with anyone because I finally had everything I ever needed. My love.

After him denying the infidelity and me choosing to believe and forgive him I ended up running into her. God's timing is the best timing. When he wants to show or tell you something he will literally rearrange the whole world so you can receive what he needs you to receive.

One night I was out with my girlfriends heartbroken because of the mess that I was in. I was high out of my mind that night but feeling good cause I had my girls with me.

We were at CVS sitting in the car in the parking lot not too far from my house. I was standing in line waiting for the customer in front of me to finish paying so that I could make my purchase. I was so under the influence I didn't even notice that she was in the same store as me. She came up to me and said, "Quaniece it's true, we have been dealing with each other the whole time you guys were together." She said he denied that we were in a relationship and continued to say we were just friends. I felt like someone stuck a knife in my heart, twisted it, and pulled it out. Not my best friend. The one that we did everything together. Who my family had loved, who I had planned on having children with, sharing my life with. I was crushed. I was humiliated and I felt betrayed. Unfortunately, not crushed enough to walk away right then and there and leave him where he stood.

Instead, I took him back and tried to act like what happened didn't happen, which was hard to do because he never stopped dealing with the girl. He created a love triangle between us. When one of us got mad he would just go right back to the other one. Until eventually, I had her number and she had mine and we would just go directly to each other to find out whatever information that was needed.

When I found out that I contracted HPV, a sexually transmitted infection that may or may not cause warts in various parts of the body, I was livid. I called her and told her. She informed me that she had already received her diagnosis and told him to tell me. Of course, he didn't.

Why didn't I walk away and leave him after his betrayal? I still wanted to change him. After numerous casual encounters and never being taken seriously, I thought he was my last hope. I didn't want to let go. I couldn't let go. Until finally one of us gave up. She left him. At that point I finally had relief. I thought that it was finally over and that I won. Until one girl turned into another. Then that girl turned into another. Until my self-esteem was so low that I didn't even care that he was cheating on me. I just didn't want him to leave me, and I wouldn't survive if he left me. He was my everything. I was addicted to the chaos, dysfunction, and confusion.

We went back and forth in our toxic environment for a while, still trying to make it work. Breaking up to making up. I did several pop-ups at his house or job oftentimes catching him with other females. Then we would have make-up sex all to get into a fight about the same thing all over again. My self-esteem was low. My insecurity was higher. I had to be with him every minute of the day. When he wasn't with me he had better be at work, or else he would hear my mouth. At that point, he used to just make up dumb arguments and do stuff to make me upset so I would get mad at him and not talk to him for a few days so he could go do whatever he wanted to do. Until he finally broke up with me.

When he broke up with me my entire world was crushed. How could he break up with me when he was the one that had put me through so much? That wasn't fair.

At the time I was in nursing school, one of the busiest times of my life. I didn't talk for weeks. Every time I would talk I would cry. The pain was too much. So, I just stopped talking. One day I came across a random praise and worship CD. I began to listen to this CD every day on my way to work and school. It was the only time that the pain wasn't as strong as it had been. I prayed over and over and asked God to heal my broken heart. Eventually, the pain went away. I became healed and whole again.

Of course, he must have sensed that I was happy and living my life without him like exes tend to do. He called me apologizing saying he wanted to make it work. He was changed and ready to be everything I ever needed him to be. Lord knows I shouldn't have given him another chance. But I still loved him. I still believed he was the right person for me even with all of the chaos and dysfunction. I wanted to show him everything I had learned about self-love in hopes that he would do the work for his own self-love. He wasn't ready. He just wasn't willing to do the work or even take accountability for his part in the toxicity of our relationship. Instead of trusting my gut and ignoring my own intuition, I tried again with him knowing that it wouldn't last. I was no longer the same person before our breakup and certain things I just wasn't standing for.

He finally told me he didn't believe in God. I think that hurt more than him cheating on me. How could we ever get married if he didn't believe in God? There was no way it was going to work.

The toxicity of our relationship turned into a struggle about infidelity to a full-blown spiritual war. Him trying to convince me that God was man-made, and me trying to prove him wrong. The exhaustion I felt from the nonstop battle between us wore me out.

I'll never forget the last fight we had. It was about religion and all kinds of conspiracy theories. The crazy thing about the whole fight was I was too tired to even argue with him. So I just let him talk. I think he was madder at me for choosing not to argue back or engage in his foolishness versus when I would let him rob me of all my energy. I tried to leave the house because I knew with our history where it could go, and I knew better. He was so upset about me leaving. I ran outside and he chased me around the car. I recall laying on my back on the hood of the car with his arms around my neck, choking me. I didn't recognize who he was. I knew he wasn't my best friend or the man I had fallen in love with. I began to have an out-of-body experience. It was like I was looking down on myself as he was choking me and saying is this really the person you want to be with? Is this really how you want to live your life? He immediately stopped choking me, and talked me into going back into the house again. I stayed the night with him but didn't sleep at all. I couldn't. I was too afraid. The next morning when he got in the shower, I got up and got dressed. I left and I never looked back. He never reached out to me. I never reached out to him. Three years went by before I saw him again.

Everything happens for a reason. You may know the reason immediately or it may take years to be revealed. But just know God makes no mistakes. You are exactly where you are supposed to be. It may not look like it, you may not feel like it, but things are happening around you. Things you can not see. In these times is where we have to trust God the most. Trust that although it may not look like the situation will ever get better, I just have to trust God and believe his promises. I have to believe that no matter what everything will work out for my good.

Never Let Me Drown

"A friend loves at at all times, and a brother is born for a time of adversity." Proverbs 17:17

Making friends was something that I never really felt comfortable doing until I reached adulthood. I wasn't the most confident person. I would usually end up with friends by being approached or through a common person. I was very shy and to myself and to be honest I never really felt that I belonged, so I never knew who to befriend. I never quite fit in with the popular confident girls, but I was too pretty and cool to be considered unpopular so I remained in this space where I was around but in the background. I was merely just existing. This is another example of not knowing who you are. You gravitate to wherever you receive attention. Sometimes you gravitate to places that should have never been blessed with your presence. I learned this the hard way. The first time I stayed friends with someone longer than I should have was in the seventh grade. She befriended me because I was the new girl at the school. I remember one morning in our home room she randomly offered me some of her lotion. Without thinking anything of it I used it and went on about my day. By the end of the day, I was called down to the principal's office only to find out that the lotion she had given me had urine in it. Another kid in our grade stole her lotion bottled peed in it and gave it back to her, and she then gave it to me. I know now that every invitation is not genuine.

At this point in my life, I take friendship very seriously. Friendship is valuable. Today, I cherish friendship in a new way. To have a good friend, one must be a good friend. The truth of that matter is I have not always been a good friend. Relationships are about learning and sometimes we have to make mistakes before we get it. Sometimes everyone has to leave and the ones who remain are the ones who get a seat at the table.

When you have been hurt you develop trust issues. When you have trust issues you can never be fully present in the relationships that you have. Friendships are definitely relationships. Yes, I was able to function and maintain friendships but when I became afraid or conflict would occur I would distance myself, not knowing that any relationship, even the best, ones will have some form of conflict somewhere.

We are all created differently with different personalities and characteristics. That is why when others are different from us or have a difference of opinion we must take a moment to stop and take in what could be a learning and/or teaching moment.

I was very good at avoiding conflict. Avoiding conflict kept me safe, because in my mind if I didn't acknowledge it, it wasn't happening. Avoiding conflict kept me in the false reality that nothing was wrong. If nothing was wrong I wouldn't have to address the issue and how the issue affected me, and boy did I have a hard time expressing myself and what my needs were. I had a habit of avoiding my negative and sad feelings, instead of allowing myself to feel and process whatever emotion that was brought up. I now know that just because I act like what I'm feeling isn't real, that doesn't mean that it goes away. It is scientifically proven that emotions carry energy and energy is stored in the body. If we do not release our emotions we carry them. This is why I am such a strong advocate for talk therapy, or just releasing what you are feeling. Keeping feelings and thoughts in your head is detrimental. I know that this may seem easier said than done, and for those who are completely against talk therapy, try purchasing a journal. Writing has been my form of therapy for a very long time. With a personal journal, no one can judge you or give you advice that you may not be ready to hear. Journaling also keeps a record of what you may be feeling and at what times as well as a way to look back and reflect. For example, when I don't feel good or I feel unmotivated or stuck, I use my feelings as a messenger. What am I thinking about that may be causing my body to feel or respond like this? Writing heals the soul. Before you know it you will have pages and pages filled with your feelings and thoughts. I'm sure there is a book inside of you. There is a book inside of all of us. Take the risk and share your story!

"Walk with the wise and become wise, for a companion of fools suffers harm." Proverbs 13:20

I often heard the saying that when you are growing you go through periods of time where you feel alone. Nothing looks or feels familiar. The people you thought would be there at the table with you when it was all said and done are no longer there to celebrate your wins. The people who turned from friends into family, not through blood but through good times and bad times. Through hard times and struggles. The one person you knew you would always be able to count on. What do you do when you lose that person? I lost my person. I can sit and go back and forth about last conversations, who was right and who was wrong, but in the end when it comes to someone that you really love none of that matters. Forgiveness and love go hand and hand. We as humans are going to make mistakes and screw up. We are going to disappoint our loved ones, our children, our friends, our parents.

I grew up with him, from school-age years all the way through adulthood. We both have seen each other evolve over and over and over again. In my heart, I truly believe that we both needed to grow separately to really evolve into the people that God intended for us to be. What started off as a small misunderstanding turned into me listening to my spirit telling me to separate myself, even though I was hurting and I knew that he would be hurt too. I almost didn't know if I would be able to function without having that love and security he provided that I had grown used to. He was my comfort. He was my peace. As I look back I think separation was God's plan all along. God is a jealous God. Where I would run to my friend for comfort I now run to God. When I have good news I now shout and thank God, because he is my supplier. When I'm struggling and afraid I call on God. He is my strength. My peace. My way maker.

God needed to separate me from those that I was tied to so that I could know that it wouldn't be anyone else but God. He needed me to take my pain and hurt to him, not another man. He needed me to rely on him for my healing and to become whole. So I did. Days turned into weeks and weeks turned into months, and each day

I began to become stronger. Within myself. With God. I was finally walking into my own power. More often than not your growth, your level up is on the other side of your comfort zone. And I have to be honest climbing to that other side is hard. It's uncomfortable. But the only person stopping you is you.

New Balance

I met my son's father at a very unique point in my life. At the time, I was in a relationship with someone that I wasn't really happy with, but he looked good on paper. He was educated, had a career, and able to provide. He was a strong black man with no record and a good job. What more could I want? According to those around me I had hit the jackpot, but I didn't feel like it. A part of me always felt that something was missing and something was lacking. But because I thought I had everything that I could want, I chose not to question what I felt. Something I feel that women do so much. We ignore our intuition and talk ourselves out of that nagging feeling we get when we know something isn't right. I think the reason for this is the fact that we as women have a hard time trusting ourselves. So many times do we ignore those red flags and feelings that we get that tells us to run the other way. Each time we ignore our intuition we tell our body that it can't trust itself. God created your intuition as a guide. As a human being it is an instinct to be able to sense danger and threat. When we ignore that, we tell our bodies and brain that we will not protect ourselves when threatened. Your body has a memory. Just because you chose to ignore doesn't mean that your body didn't store this information. How we operate is almost habitual and synchronized. Humans are very much creatures of habits.

I was completely unhappy and I was resentful. Not only was I unhappy in my relationship, day by day I was beginning to hate and resent my career. Every time I could find a reason to get angry or irritated I did. Every time I could find a way to hurt my boyfriend's feelings I did. I wanted him to feel the unhappiness that I was feeling. I was resentful and bitter and I felt stuck. I felt robbed. I felt robbed because I did everything the way I was told I was supposed to, yet I still was unhappy. I did everything right. I did everything they told me to do. But what about Quaniece? What about what I wanted and what I needed? I lacked love. I was looking for a deeper love. A fulfilling love. Something that I thought was going to fill this void that I felt in my heart.

To get out of this funk I felt like I needed to do something that I had never done. So I decided to take a trip with my girlfriends and go to Miami for my birthday. This trip changed my life. One experience has the power to change your entire life. While on this trip I linked up with a guy who I would have never thought would become the soul I shared my child with.

My son's father was someone I had already known from back home, it just so happened that we were on vacation at the same time in the same city. Both of us were in Miami celebrating our birthdays. When I decided to link up with him I didn't think much of it, but it was something about our interaction and energy that was very different than what it usually was when I saw him back home. I was experiencing things that I don't think I'd ever experienced before. Feelings that I never really felt before. He felt familiar and I felt entirely too comfortable. After all that I been through when it came to the opposite sex, my guard was up. I didn't just trust anyone with handling the care of my heart and emotions. But he was able to bypass that. We talked for hours on the balcony about everything, revealing my insecurities to him just to see how he would respond. I was in a whole relationship and couldn't even share these things with my boyfriend. For every negative thing I had to say about myself, he said something uplifting and loving to say to. I didn't like what I saw when I looked in the mirror and he told me so many times how everything about me was perfect and amazing. I remember at the time wishing that I was able to see what he saw. But I just couldn't. When I looked into the mirror I hated what I saw. I knew that I was a good catch, I knew that I brought a lot to the table, but I wanted someone to see me for me. Not for what I have accomplished in life, but for me. The real me. At the time my thoughts were, "If you are so amazing why can't you keep friends? Why do guys love you and then leave you sometimes with no explanation?" I wanted someone to choose and love me. My need for outside validation was eating me alive. With him I felt loved, I felt honored, I felt seen. He saw me before I saw myself. After experiencing that, there was no way I was going to be able to go home and return to my regular life. South Beach is a place that I will forever hold close to my heart. Going on this trip awakened my soul. For so long I felt like everyone was in control of my life. This trip gave me a taste of what could happen if I just let go of what everyone else wanted me to do and be. This trip was when I made the decision to never live in bondage again.

I know you probably are wondering how it went down when I went home right? I know, just messy. Upon returning home to my boyfriend, I went to his apartment. Technically it was still my birthday and I was still celebrating. After celebrating for the night when I woke up the next morning I remember laying in his bed turning over and seeing makeup on his pillowcases. My heart stopped, but it wasn't a pain that stopped it. I felt relief. I didn't have to carry around the burden of being unfaithful. The evidence of us both being unhappy was there on the sheets. The real question I should have asked myself was if you know you are unhappy, why is there a need for evidence? Why be in a place where you know you aren't happy, and clearly he felt the same way? The truth of the matter is I knew at that moment I wouldn't be in the relationship much longer. My mind had changed and I had experienced something different. I didn't want to prove to him anymore why he should treat me like a Queen. I didn't want to beg him to see me anymore. I just didn't have the courage to tell him I no longer wanted to try anymore.

God knows the desires of our hearts because he gives them to us. I desired to be released from this relationship. Fear was keeping me from moving. The fear of the unknown. The fear of facing the fact that I had been in another failed relationship. I was afraid of ending up alone. The shame from the revelation that I had failed at yet another relationship kept me from moving. If I didn't leave even though my soul was aching to go, it would feed the belief system that was implanted in me. That I am unlovable and no one would ever be happy with me. That I was bad at relationships, and even though I had worked at becoming a better person none of what I knew mattered because I still made the wrong choice. The enemy's attack on my mind has kept me stuck and in endless cycles year after year, without me even knowing. One of those cycles was being silent about my suffering. Keeping all my pain on the inside of me. The more silent that I was the more resentment began to build in my heart. God can't bless a bitter heart. At the time, I didn't know that. I didn't know that what is in the root of your heart becomes revealed in the way that you speak to yourself and to others. There was a lot of hatred in my heart, self-hatred.

One day he called me and asked if he could come over so we could talk. I thought that this was needed, being that I had returned from vacation over a month ago and nothing got better between us. If anything, it was getting worse and worse. So I agreed to the conversation that we both were trying to ignore but one of us finally got the courage to say something. My boyfriend at the time came over to tell me that he loved me very much, and I was everything that he wanted in a woman. But there was a reason that he was always holding himself back from showing me the love and affection that I was begging him for. He told me since the beginning of us dating, which had been over a year at this point, he had been uncomfortable with the way my vagina smells when we engaged in sexual intercourse. What blew my mind about this conversation wasn't about what he said. It was more about the fact that for over a year he didn't tell me. That was the ultimate betrayal. For over a year he dangled his love in front of me and every time I jumped up to grab it he would snatch it away. For over a year he had convinced me that he wasn't a loving and affectionate person. That expressing himself just wasn't his thing. He even went as far as to tell me that he grew up in a household where his parents never told him that they loved him. I felt his pain, and I wanted to love it away. I felt his pain and I wanted to pour all my love into his hurt. So when he came to me with this information I just couldn't believe it. The person who always preached to me the importance of never making yourself uncomfortable to make another person comfortable had in fact been uncomfortable. Any respect I had for him went out the window. I wasn't angry; I was more disappointed with the time lost that I invested in the relationship, especially regarding something that we both had the power to fix with a simple conversation. Had I known, I could have made an appointment with the doctor to find out what was wrong. Being that we both were healthcare professionals, his first thought should have been something is wrong and I love her so I want to help her fix it. Not intentionally withhold love and affection from her to punish her. I remember crying after he broke up with me that night. I told myself that I would allow myself to cry and feel for that night but the next day I was going to start over. I was going to focus on me. The truth of the matter was that he did me a favor by breaking up with me. I didn't have enough courage to leave the relationship, so God gave me an out. He made a way for me to move when I didn't have the strength to do so myself.

I actually found out that I did have a recurring bacterial infection, which was an indicator that my body was rejecting his. We were never supposed to be from the get-go. Ladies, our most intimate parts are exactly that, intimate. We have to be careful who we allow in our most private places. Not just physically, but spiritually as well.

Speak

"You get in life what you have the courage to ask for." –

Oprah Winfrey

Before becoming my son's father, he was my "McSavage." I say Mc because I am a huge Grey's Anatomy fan and when you know you just know. He was bold and fearless, the opposite of my usual safe choice. I never dated popular guys or guys that many women flocked to. I always went for the quiet one. The one unseen, or blending in with the background. He was none of that. I say that to say he was one of the first choices I made by stepping out and just going with how I felt. I didn't have a plan, nor did I have any answers. I just knew that for my entire life I did and said what I was supposed to. For the first time in my life, I didn't have to worry. With him, I felt free and unbound. I didn't have the pressure of having to be perfect. I could finally be me. No performance needed. He accepted me for who I was as I was. Acceptance from someone was what I had desperately needed. I just needed someone to see me and he did, and it made me feel loved and alive. I finally felt in control over myself, until I didn't. Our arrangement went on for almost two years before I found myself pregnant. This is where it got real and I had to put on my big girl shoes.

When I found out I was pregnant the reality of my situation hit me like a ton of bricks. I was pregnant by someone who I wasn't even in a relationship with. Someone who was tied to two other women that he had children with. I had real grown-up problems that I needed to handle and address, and I wasn't ready to fully deal with that head-on so I did what I did best— avoid but only for so long.

I knew it was certain, this guy was going to be in my life for the rest of my life and that scared me. Big time. My track record showed me to be a runner. Running is what I did when things got hard or I became uncomfortable. Life is so much easier when you only have yourself to think or worry about. But is it really? My answer is different now cause I've lived through it. But at this time, I was beyond afraid and ashamed. I was ashamed of the fact that I waited so long and took pride in how many years of being free of children. Now I wouldn't be. I had dreams. I had a future. I had things that I still wanted to accomplish. How am I going to be able to do all of this and still be someone's mother? But beyond my aspirations for my career, I had dreams of becoming a mother under the condition of being someone's wife. The man that God had for me. Not this way. I was extremely hard on myself. It was at this point that I was really humbled. Everything I thought that I would never be in one moment I became. God has a way of humbling us. The very same people that we think we could never be, we can become. We do things that we think we may never do. Life has no rules and no one is exempt from any experience. It can be you. It was me.

With God all things are possible. I had to live through this to know. I accepted the reality of my situation with the belief that I would still be able to accomplish my goals as a single mother. Yes I may have to work harder and it may take longer, but I will get there. Every day I began to play "To Zion," a song by Lauryn Hill dedicated to her first son. This song gave me comfort. I had to believe that what God placed inside of my womb would bless me, even though I couldn't see it at the time. I had to believe and trust that God would make sure that my baby and I would be alright like he had done for me all these other times. As you can see I am living proof that he did. Not only did he clear the path for me, but he healed me and made me whole so that in turn I would be able to turn around and help someone else.

Maybe your situation is not the transition to becoming a parent. Maybe it's leaving a relationship, or a career, or moving across the country. Maybe it's getting married, or starting the business. All things that are new can be scary to do at first. But with God, you don't have to live in fear. In fact, the closer my relationship with God became, the less fear I felt.

"Have I not commanded you? Be strong and courageous. Do not be afraid; do not be discouraged, for the LORD your God will be with you wherever you go." Joshua 1:9

I made it through my pregnancy with my head held up the best way I knew how. I took as many pictures and videos as I could. My focus became my health and mental health as well as my child's health. I made the decision to not bother myself with the burden of worrying about my son's father and his preparation for our son's arrival. My only concern was being the best mother that I could be for my innocent child and getting my child here safely. I also knew I had to be in the best place that I could so that I wouldn't be trying to fill my child up from an empty vessel.

After the birth of my son, the relationship that I had with his father became quite cloudy. It was a very hard and confusing period for me. For a long time, I was in denial about my feelings for him. I tried to act as if not being together didn't affect me and ignored the pain I felt in my chest every time someone asked me if I was in a relationship with my child's father. I would say no, but then say we have a great relationship. Well, if our relationship was so great what was stopping us from being together? If we loved each other so much why couldn't we be together? I acted as if I was okay with the dynamic of our relationship. The truth is for a while it was until it wasn't. Avoiding intimacy was my pattern and I felt a lot more deeply for him than I wanted to admit. My truth is that I had always been in love with him. But I was too afraid, afraid of becoming close to someone again, afraid of rejection, afraid of asking for what I wanted, afraid of the unknown. I wanted to give love another try but I never wanted to experience the pain I felt after my heart was broken by my best friend. So I fought my feelings or acted as if they weren't there. For the most part, I kept my feelings under control, or so I thought. The real tea is I was brewing inside. I was filled with anger and resentment at myself because I was suffering and I was too afraid to ask for what I desired. I could only blame myself. For so long I remained silent, feeling like I didn't have the right to ask for my needs to be met. I felt like because the relationship started out one way that I couldn't change my mind. I blamed myself for getting into this, and I was angry because I didn't know how to get out. I thank God for his grace and mercy every day. Yes, I may have gotten myself into this situation, but God's love freed me, and he didn't hold anything from my past against me. Your past does not define you. It was what you needed at that time to become who God has called you to be. God wants to prune you. He wants to build your strength and character. He wants you to trust in him at all times. He wants you to know that you can try to do it alone but it won't last you will grow weary. God gives you rest. He refreshes you. He gives you strength and power. He wants you to know no matter what you face, no matter what you are up against, with him, you are victorious.

"For everyone born of God overcomes the world. This is the victory that has overcome the world, even our faith." 1John 5:4

Shortly after my son's first birthday is when it all hit the fan. I began to drink. I indulged in alcohol before but alcohol was never my go-to. My favorite has always been the ganja. But with alcohol, I felt different. I loved the feeling that alcohol gave me. It made me bold. It made me fearless. Alcohol was literally my liquid courage.

One night at a bar after having way too many drinks, I got into an altercation. One that changed my life. I had finally come face to face with my son's father's oldest son's mother that he was currently living with. To some, "baby mamas" arguing in a bar is normal. But for me, it was one of the most humiliating experiences I had ever been a part of. Not because we got into a screaming match at a bar, but because I completely lost it. I take a lot of pride in being a woman who always had herself under control. I have been a professional since the age of 22. I was someone's nurse in a public place acting a fool. I could have lost everything that night. All for what? A man? Quaniece would never conduct herself that way. What had I allowed myself to turn into? My behavior that night was disgusting. God had seen that I was spiraling out of control and he needed to get my attention. He needed to snap me out of this false reality that I had been living in. He needed me to take back my power.

It was after this moment that I knew that I had to change. The way that I was living I couldn't do it for another day. My life had become filled with lies, secrets, and shame. Somewhere over the last two years I completely lost myself. Conversations I wanted to avoid, feelings that I didn't want to acknowledge all contributed to the fact that I was living a life that I didn't want anymore.

As much as I loved my son's father, I knew that with the way that things were going this would never work. To know that there could be somebody out there who loved me for me, without the baggage. Without the hurt. Without all the tears. I loved him, but I loved me more. I loved him but I wanted my peace more. I wanted my son to have both of his parents together in a healthy and loving relationship. That was my desire. Not this circus that my life had turned into, and not at the expense of my own peace and joy. There had to be more. I desired someone to treat and put me first. I was so tired of being put on the back burner. By everyone. I was tired of feeling less than. Tired of going above and beyond and getting the bare minimum in return. I had officially reached my breaking point. So I gave up. I had to believe that there was strength on the other side of my pain. I had to believe that there would be sun on the other side of all this gloom and rain. I just had to believe and trust in God. I had to believe that God knows each and every desire in my heart. He knows what I need. I had to believe and trust that he would provide for me. What's the point in being with someone when you feel like you have to be everything all on your own? I can do bad by myself. It was bigger than just me at this point in my life.

See before, I didn't have a son watching me. A son depending on me to be healed and whole. A son that wouldn't remember his mom in tears and sad. When I look in my son's eyes and see his smile I have to remember who I am doing this for. I have to remember that this life is bigger than just me. The pressure to do better because I know better was at an all-time high. I couldn't play anymore like my heart and feelings were a game. My feelings are valid and they matter. My needs were valid and they matter. I had to love me more than I loved him because loving him was killing me. Loving him was holding me back from everything that I had seen in my future. Not because he was a bad person, but because of how I felt when I was with him. Gone are the days where I surround myself around anyone or anything who makes me feel less than or makes me question my worth. I now know who I belong to.

It got a lot worse before it got better. The incident at the bar led me to want to develop a closer relationship with God. So that's what I did. I started going back to church and allowing God to work on me and heal me. But as I got closer to God my attacks got heavier and heavier. Until I finally surrendered, prayed, and took it to God. I asked God to let his will be done, and not mine. When I invited God into the relationship with my son's father over time things changed. Where I would complain and vent to those around me, I began to pray. I no longer go to others when I am offended or hurt. I go to God. God has become my confidant, my best friend, my everything. Had it not been for this chaotic time in my life I would never have never surrendered myself to him. I truly believe that this is the reason for me enduring what I did at this period of time in my life. You will continue to relive and recreate the same scenarios in life over and over again until you fully embrace the lesson. There was something that I needed to leave behind. A part of me that God no longer wanted me to identify myself with. No longer was I the girl that just accepted what she was given. No longer was I the girl that sacrificed her self-worth for others. It was time for me to not only know how to love myself but apply the knowledge that I have learned. Knowledge is power, don't get me wrong, but if you don't apply what you know, that knowledge is useless. I needed God's help to fix this. I needed strength and discipline to stick to what I knew that I deserved and not budge no matter how much it hurt.

God's love and grace saved, restored, and renewed my relationship with my son's father. God had to come and wreck what we set in motion before what we set in motion wrecked us. God will never put more on you than you can handle. The truth was that my son's father and I were madly in love with each other, but we both were severely damaged and broken. After the turmoil that had taken place, our relationship would never work without something bigger involved.

Where I thought that I would never be able to forgive, God bounded up those wounds. While healing, I weighed my options and went back and forth with myself for months and months. Suffering in the process. Battling my pride. Battling my ego. The time we spent apart really showed me how much I wanted him in my life. How much I wanted to make our family work. The heart desires what the heart desires, and for a while, I let my pride win while silently suffering. I didn't want to be the weak girl who forgives. Not Quaniece. The person who prided herself on loving herself. But the reality is I was holding myself up to this imaginary standard of being perfect, and the truth is that I am human. My soul is in a human body, having a human experience. Mistakes and pain are a part of our experience. But so is love, joy, forgiveness, and peace. I made the decision to forgive myself for what I allowed to have happened in the past because God had already forgiven me before it even happened. I also made the decision to forgive my son's father. This led to both of us deciding to give our relationship a chance. Day by day we practiced better communication, we learned to communicate about our fears and unhealed baggage that was leaking into the relationship. Couples therapy and individual therapy paired with a lot of prayer gave us the strength that we both needed to try to fight for our relationship together versus apart. You have to do the work, and with the right person, it's worth it.

I can honestly say when God told me that one night to release him I was so afraid I was afraid that it was really going to be over for good. But I was obedient and I listened. I was willing to let go of whatever God told me to gain peace, and I am happy that I did.

I've learned on this journey that people don't belong to us. God simply loans us our loved ones. That's why we must cherish the moments that we do have. If it's meant for you it will come back, but even if it doesn't, that doesn't make the experience any less valuable, and it certainly doesn't make you less lovable. You will always be worth it.

Only The Guilty Get Offended

The opinions of others and what they thought of me often kept me stuck. It was hard for me to make a decision on anything because I always felt that I was being judged. With a background like mine, I always felt insecure. Word of advice: you can't care what anyone thinks. You have to get comfortable with not being liked. When you are living your truth that can sometimes stir up jealousy or insecurities in others. Shine anyway. In the past, I was afraid of shining because I didn't want to make others around me uncomfortable. The truth is God created you to shine. Allow God's light to shine through you in whichever way he gifted you to do. You have the power to create the life that you want. Make sure that it's a life that you want to live and not others around you. Make sure that it's a life that gives you fulfillment and joy. You have to be ok with the decisions you make. Live your life for you.

Favor Ain't Fair

I've struggled with speaking up for myself my entire life. I now know that this upbringing was intentional. It was intentional for me to be silenced so that I could understand the value of words and speaking life into others and myself. The war that the enemy placed on my voice was because he knew what my gifts were and what God had placed down on the inside of me. This book is a product of what God had placed down on the inside of me. If it was up to me, I would have never gotten around to writing this book. I am just a vessel that God is using. What the enemy used to try to destroy me, God used it for his good. I will never forget the suffering that I endured in silence. The silent battles that I fought. Those tears that I cried in silence because I felt as if I deserved my suffering. Those seasons of being overlooked and hidden. We call that a wilderness season. God brought me out of my wilderness season. I am stronger and I am wiser. No longer do I cower or run from conflict or allow fear to keep me paralyzed. I know that God is with me and that the battle is not mine. I know who I can call on when I need strength and wisdom. I believe in the power that he has placed in me. Now, you must believe in the power that he has placed in YOU.

"But unto each one of us was the grace given according to the measure of the gift of Christ." Ephesians 4:7

As I finish this book, I hope you are left with something that has the ability to change your life. I hope through my mess you were able to see beyond the surface and dig deeper to actually receive this message. My message was intended for you to know who God is and the grace that he has gifted to all of us. Where you have been it doesn't matter. Sins cancelled. Pain from the past, silently suffering, guilt, depression, anxiety, thoughts that never cease to stop none of that matters. I've endured molestation, rape, shame, fear, doubt, domestic violence, and substance abuse. But I am still standing. God still used me. Little old me from a small town called Windsor in Connecticut. I remember the times in my life where I thought God didn't know I existed. He didn't know the girl that let people use and walk all over her. He didn't know the girl who always had a smile on her face but was secretly dying inside. He didn't know the girl who thought maybe if I just disappeared someone would notice me. He didn't know the girl that was always there but never chosen or noticed. God couldn't possibly know who I was because he wouldn't have let me suffer this long. The truth was while I was going through all of those times not only did God never leave me but he was there with me the whole time. He actually went ahead of me and cleared my path so many times. So many dark moments and days, so much pain. I never thought that I would see a light at the end of the tunnel. But there is light. In all dark areas there is light. For me, that light was God's love. Through God's light and love, a better me was produced.

Whatever you are going through and wherever you are at this moment I want you to know that a better you is on the other side of whatever it is that you're fighting. A side of you that is beyond your imagination. A side of you so grand that it probably scares you and it should, because you can't get there without God. God has placed things on the inside of you that needs to be birthed through you, and the only person who can do it the way you can is you. So stop now. Stop trying to be like someone else. Stop seeking validation from those around you and look to God. He created you. He had plans for you while you were in your mother's womb. You are loved and you are so very important. You are a part of God's plan and design. You are needed. See beyond what you may currently feel about yourself, and ask God for the ability to see yourself through his eyes. If you saw yourself through his eyes you would know how significant you are to him. How significant you are to this world. You belong here.

We all are born with the emotional need for love, significance, and security. We are born with these needs. You are not wrong for wanting these things. In fact, you are doing yourself a disservice by denying yourself of these things. I thought that I was wrong for needing and wanting these things. It made me feel weak. In a society that constantly tells women that we are crazy, angry, or bitter for speaking out for what we want. That we are too emotional and unable to lead. Queens, our needs aren't invalid or wrong, however, I can only speak for myself and see the error in where I was looking to get those needs fulfilled. I was suffering because I was seeking to be filled by a source that only God has the capacity to fill. Humans, we will always fall short.

As I minister to you, I minister to myself because every day I still have to remind myself when my thoughts begin to race. When I began to sink back into those habits and patterns that no longer serve me. When I let my crown slip a little bit, this is a reminder to you that even if you may let your crown slip a little bit you are still a Queen, it is your inheritance. Nothing you do or don't do will ever be able to change that. There is nothing that will ever be able to separate you from the love that God has over you, your life and his promises.

Made in the USA
Middletown, DE
23 June 2020

97890238R00085